"If you are struggling with BDD, you need to understand what it is and your options for dealing with it in a concise and practical way. This book will help you explore all of the major approaches that have shown to be helpful. Whether you are going into therapy or want to address this problem on your own, you will find value on every page."

—Steven C. Hayes, professor of psychology at University of Nevada, and author of *Get Out of Your Mind and Into Your Life*

"In this age where, sadly, so many people are unhappy with their appearance, this book becomes a close friend who completely understands all aspects of true BDD and really can help you on the road to a better life."

—Stephen Westwood, author of *Body Dysmorphic Disorder: A Memoir*, and *Suicide Junkie*

"Anyone who struggles with body dysmorphic disorder should make sure to read this book. Fugen Neziroglu has written an easy-to-read book that distills the core features of overcoming BDD."

—David Veale, MD, author of *Overcoming Body Image Problems*

D0841410

"Body dysmorphic disorder can be a relentlessly tormenting disorder, too often misunderstood by even those in the mental health profession. People who have it often experience a tremendous sense of shame while living with considerable despair and hopelessness. *Overcoming Body Dysmorphic Disorder* clearly demonstrates, however, that there is in fact reason for hope. The authors have put together a carefully crafted self-help manual, complete with strategies to guide those with BDD through their recovery. Cognitive-behavioral therapy, exposure therapy, ACT, and task concentration skills are all thoroughly explored in an effective, easy-to-read manner that is useful for patients and therapists alike."

—Scott M. Granet, LCSW, director at the OCD-BDD Clinic of Northern California

"*Overcoming Body Dysmorphic Disorder* is more than a book; it is a must-have companion for anyone ready for life after BDD. Whether you are suffering in silence or already working with a licensed therapist, this book will assist you in your recovery. The compassionate authors offer a holistic approach, tackling BDD from every angle and providing easy-to-follow, effective exercises to improve your quality of life and defeat BDD. What I love most about this book is it offers *solutions*."

—Brit Brimhall, director of BDD Central

OVERCOMING BODY DYSMORPHIC DISORDER

A Cognitive Behavioral Approach to Reclaiming Your Life

FUGEN NEZIROGLU, PhD
SONY KHEMLANI-PATEL, PhD
MELANIE T. SANTOS, PsyD

New Harbinger Publications, Inc.

Publisher's Note

Distributed in Canada by Raincoast Books

Copyright © 2012 by Fugen Neziroglu, Sony Khemlani-Patel,
              & Melanie T. Santos
              New Harbinger Publications, Inc.
              5674 Shattuck Avenue
              Oakland, CA 94609
              www.newharbinger.com

Cover design by Amy Shoup
Text design by Tracy Marie Carlson
Acquired by Catharine Meyers
Edited by Jean Blomquist

Library of Congress Cataloging-in-Publication Data

Neziroglu, Fugen.

  Overcoming body dysmorphic disorder : a cognitive behavioral approach to reclaiming your life / Fugen Neziroglu, Sony Khemlani-Petal, Melanie T. Santos.

    p. cm.

  Summary: "Overcoming Body Dysmorphic Disorder offers BDD individuals a practical guide to the mindfulness, acceptance, and exposure and response prevention strategies that can help them overcome the disorder. Presented by lead author Fugen Neziroglu, an anxiety expert regularly featured on A&E's television show Hoarders, this comprehensive guide offers self-assessment tools and a complete cognitive behavioral therapy (CBT) program for reducing the effect of BDD on sufferers' lives. Its step-by-step guidance and easy-to-follow exercises are sure to help readers with BDD move beyond their anxieties and start living with greater freedom and confidence than ever before"-- Provided by publisher.

  Includes bibliographical references.

  ISBN 978-1-60882-149-5 (pbk.) -- ISBN 978-1-60882-150-1 (pdf e-book) -- ISBN 978-1-60882-151-8 (epub)

  1. Body dysmorphic disorder--Treatment. 2. Cognitive therapy. I. Khemlani-Petal, Sony. II. Santos, Melanie T. III. Title.

  RC569.5.B64N49 2012

  616.89'1425--dc23

                        2012014999

Printed in the United States of America

14   13   12

10 9 8 7 6 5 4 3 2 1   First printing

Contents

Introduction

Do you feel conflicted about purchasing this book? Have you been at war with your body and mind for some time? Perhaps you spend countless hours looking in the mirror and hoping another reflection will stare back at you. Maybe you've been to an endless string of therapists or medical professionals without any improvement in the way you feel. So, searching for some answers and relief, you picked up this book. Perhaps you're skeptical about the diagnosis of body dysmorphic disorder (BDD), but you want to learn more—or prove to others that you don't have it! Or maybe a family member or friend bought this book for you and it's been lying unopened on your bedside table for months because you just couldn't open it—until now. Perhaps, after diagnosing yourself, you ordered the book online because you preferred the safety of receiving it by mail rather than face the potential embarrassment and anxiety of buying it in a bookstore. No matter how or why you acquired *Overcoming BDD*, we suspect that you want your life to be better than it currently is. If these thoughts and experiences sound familiar, you are not alone! Body dysmorphic disorder (BDD) can be an extremely difficult disorder to live with. Not only will this book help you better understand BDD, it also will give you many strategies to help you overcome it. We hope this book will give you the answers and peace of mind that you seek.

Defining Body Dysmorphic Disorder

Body dysmorphic disorder (BDD) was initially identified in the 1800s by Enrico Morselli, an Italian physician. Very little information existed about BDD in the psychiatric literature until more than one hundred years later. Since then, thanks to a small group of very dedicated researchers, we can confidently identify and treat it successfully. Mental health professionals define *body dysmorphic disorder* (BDD) as a preoccupation with a perceived or minor flaw in appearance. If a minor flaw does exist, the amount of distress it causes is above and beyond what might normally be expected. The preoccupation leads to a significant degree of distress and interference in daily life. If you have BDD, you are likely to avoid certain situations that make you anxious, such as being seen in a bathing suit or talking close up to someone. We'll go into detail in the next few chapters about the types of situations most people avoid and why. When you're not avoiding, you may try to hide the part of your body that you feel uncomfortable with. For example, you may wear a cap to hide your hairline or you may use makeup to hide your blemishes. Although facial features are the most commonly targeted area, any body part can be the focus.

Since most human beings hold strong opinions about their appearance and, unfortunately, a majority of the public is dissatisfied with some aspect of their appearance, you may wonder how we differentiate BDD from normal concerns. The main difference lies in the amount of time you spend thinking about your looks and trying to find ways to deal with your unhappiness with the way you look. For example, if you have BDD, you may think about your appearance for hours every day, while people who are merely dissatisfied with their appearance may only think about it for a few moments while getting dressed in the morning. Or you may feel compelled to get a haircut weekly to achieve a perfect hairstyle, while someone without BDD may wait six weeks after an unflattering haircut to get another cut. In short, being focused on your appearance most of the time interferes with the way you really want to spend your life. (In chapter 1, we'll give many more examples of those who are merely dissatisfied with their looks versus those who may suffer from BDD.)

BDD Behaviors

People with BDD share many similar behaviors. The common theme among all is the urge to scrutinize, improve, or hide the body part of concern. Mirror checking is the most common behavior. In fact, we've never met someone with BDD who didn't struggle daily with the mirror in some manner. Although a majority mirror check, others avoid looking at their reflection at all costs. Attempts to improve one's appearance depend upon the body part of concern. For example, if you're concerned with the color and texture of your hair, you may make frequent trips to a hair salon or use multiple hair products, which is quite common. Other common BDD behaviors include researching cosmetic surgery, comparing yourself to others, seeking reassurance from family, and skin picking.

If attempts to improve your body part of concern become increasingly frustrating or unsuccessful, you may search for ways to hide your appearance using clothing and makeup, or you may even completely avoid a variety of situations. The type and amount of situations that are avoided differ from person to person and can spiral out of control. Sadly, we've seen cases where simple activities like retrieving the mail become difficult. Typically, you avoid situations involving frequent and close contact due to the anxiety, shame, or sadness experienced. Avoidance of a situation may bring immediate relief, but in the long run it doesn't work. You will just continue to have the same bad feelings and thoughts. Short-term relief never results in long-term gains.

Life with BDD

Life with BDD varies from person to person, but there are commonalities. The following stories of Ana, Keith, Matthew, and Alicia illustrate the common struggles and features of BDD. (These stories are based on a composite of many people we've treated, and all names are fictitious.)

• Ana's Story

Ana is an eighteen-year-old, first-year college student. She took a medical leave of absence from school due to an increase in her BDD and social phobia symptoms. Her social phobia has been noticeable since kindergarten; she was always labeled the "shy" kid in her class. She first experienced BDD symptoms, which she initially kept secret from friends and family, in seventh grade. Ana's main dissatisfaction was with redness and acne on her face. Her BDD symptoms worsened during her junior year of high school, and she was forced to tell her family. She mirror checked for an hour in the morning before school, used skin products to control her acne, and began picking at the acne, which created more scars. Believing they would make her skin more oily, she refused to eat any fried foods or chocolate. She washed her hands multiple times a day, especially when she was forced to touch public doorknobs or other surfaces. Because she feared aggravating her skin, she would not touch her face. She avoided anxious situations, such as attending large parties or eating lunch in a busy cafeteria, and she preferred to stay with her small group of familiar friends rather than pursue other friendships and experiences. She recalls oversleeping frequently on weekdays due to her fears of facing the day.

During her senior year, she decided to apply to colleges within a short drive from her home—she lived with her parents and younger sister—realizing that being far away would greatly increase her anxiety. In the summer before college, she convinced her reluctant parents to seek a dermatology consult. The first dermatologist didn't believe that she had a skin condition that required treatment and refused to prescribe any skin products for her. Believing the first dermatologist to be incompetent, she sought out a second dermatologist, who agreed to prescribe a topical cream.

Ana sought a consult with us after an extremely difficult first month of college. She felt depressed, hopeless, and guilty for wasting her parents' money on tuition. While aware of her depression, she clearly articulated her skepticism when we diagnosed her with BDD. She expressed her desire to be on Accutane (isotretinoin) and to find other skin procedures to correct her skin imperfections. She was not on any medications at the time.

• Keith's Story

Keith is a twenty-nine-year-old who was equally concerned with hair loss and muscularity. He believed that his hairline was receding and that his body was not muscular enough. His dissatisfaction with his appearance began at age fourteen, when he was regularly teased about his high voice and lack of facial and body hair. He was one of the last in his freshman class to hit puberty. Keith continued to be self-conscious throughout high school, but he discovered that weight lifting to build muscle led to a feeling of accomplishment and control over his appearance. In college, he began using steroids and switching from one supplement to another to achieve the maximum benefit from his daily weight training. Despite feedback from friends that he was body building excessively, Keith continued to strive for the perfect body. He also ate an excessive amount of calories a day. His concern with hair began at age twenty-five, when he learned that some of the supplements and steroids he took could lead to hair loss. He mirror checked before and after work and continued to exercise daily when he began cognitive behavioral treatment with us.

• Matthew's Story

Matthew is a forty-one-year-old divorced man who was mainly concerned with the shape and size of his nose. He believed that it didn't fit with the rest of his facial features. His symptoms began at age fifteen, after surgery for a deviated septum. He recalled being somewhat dissatisfied with his appearance prior to that, but he believed his nose looked significantly worse after the surgery. He experienced his first episode of depression at age sixteen and continued to struggle with depression throughout college. He sought psychiatric treatment in his early twenties, after he was unable to successfully maintain his job responsibilities. Medication led to an improvement of both BDD and depression symptoms, and he was able to earn a graduate degree and get married.

Matthew's symptoms returned in his early thirties, after his marriage dissolved and he discontinued medication. He researched cosmetic surgery and consulted a number of surgeons. He sought treatment with us after hospitalization due to a suicide attempt. Matthew reported that his suicidal feelings had worsened after he was turned down for cosmetic surgery. He felt hopeless and defeated when he entered treatment with us; he didn't believe that psychological treatment would be the answer to his struggle.

• Alicia's Story

Alicia is a single thirty-five-year-old who sought treatment due to her BDD. She diagnosed herself after watching a television documentary about the disorder. She had recently been dating someone seriously, which worsened her appearance concerns. Alicia was mainly concerned with her hair. She had numerous concerns with it, including the color and texture. She believed her hair color was too flat and the texture too thin. She described her hair as "limp and lifeless." She believed that her hair color also made her face appear less attractive and pale. Alicia had spent a significant amount of money on hair styling and coloring. She had collected a large number of magazines, and she spent much of her evenings comparing herself to the photos in them. She also brought the photos to the salons in order to show the style and color she desired. Her anxiety and avoidance of social situations as well her touching and looking at her hair were worse before and after she had a haircut.

Perhaps you recognize yourself in one or more of these stories. Despite their painful struggles with BDD, Ana, Keith, Matthew, and Alicia all found ways to overcome their BDD and live their lives more fully and freely. We'll return to their stories throughout the book.

How to Use This Book

We designed this book to help you understand BDD. We also offer some strategies and techniques to help you fight against BDD. We encourage you to first skim through the book from beginning to end to acquaint yourself with the disorder. Then read each chapter carefully. Doing the exercises will help you in your struggles with BDD, so we strongly encourage you to do them. Just reading through the exercises won't give you a complete understanding of the techniques or the practice required to master them. Keep a notebook and pen with you at all times to write down your feelings, thoughts, and behaviors. We include many self-assessment tools that will help you understand what you're experiencing and why.

We invite you to pay attention to how the chapters relate to you. In chapter 1, we give you a more in-depth look at BDD. We describe the symptoms and explain how normal discontent is different from BDD as well as how severity and level of insight relate to BDD. In chapter 2, using our biopsychosocial model, we explain how BDD develops. Chapter 3 discusses reasons to seek treatment, such as quality of life issues, the ineffectiveness of cosmetic and dermatological procedures, and how your loved ones are affected by your BDD. In chapter 4, we get into what to expect in treatment and how you can assess whether you have BDD. Chapters 5 through 8 consist of treatment techniques, including cognitive therapy, exposure and response prevention, attentional training, and acceptance and commitment therapy. These treatment chapters are full of exercises to assist you in conquering BDD. Relapse prevention is the focus of chapter 9. Chapter 10 is devoted to how family members can help you better manage and overcome your BDD.

At times, you may find the journey through this book difficult or intimidating. Take your time and review chapters, if needed. Above all, we encourage you to actively engage in this book by writing notes and doing the exercises. Don't be discouraged. It takes practice and repetition to learn the concepts and incorporate them into your life. The techniques we offer you *do* work. We've seen them work for many others; they can work for you as well. Progress is like a stock market ticker—ups and downs are inevitable, but in the long run, your investment will pay off.

1

What Is BDD?

Understanding Body Dysmorphic Disorder

After reading the introduction, you may be thinking that some of the symptoms of BDD could apply to anyone. After all, the beauty industry is a multibillion-dollar business. That can't all come from people with BDD. Everybody pours time and resources into enhancing their appearance. BDD is unlike other disorders because we all want to look good and, at one time or another, we've all been unhappy with some aspect of our bodies. BDD is not like anxiety and depression, which are easy to recognize and which sufferers are desperate to change. (Sometimes people with BDD don't want to change from a psychological perspective but only a physical one.) We all know that most people don't walk around feeling so anxious that they can't breathe or so depressed that they can't get themselves out of bed. However, wanting to look good, getting compliments, and being accepted are things that we all want. This is where the problem lies. How do you know if your concerns about your appearance are over the edge or just like everyone else's concerns? In this chapter, we'll explore that question. We'll first describe the range between what we call "normal discontent" and BDD. Then we'll explain the thoughts, feelings, and behaviors as well as conditions related to BDD.

Do You Have BDD?

Let's begin by looking at the symptoms of BDD. Before we go into more detail, we'd like you to complete the "Symptoms Checklist" exercise below. Most people engage in some of the behaviors on the checklist at one time or another. The difference between a person with BDD and a person without it lies in the amount of time these activities take, the urgency with which they are performed, and the overall disruption they cause in daily life.

EXERCISE: Symptoms Checklist

Please place a check before the activities in which you regularly engage as a result of your preoccupation with your body part(s) of concern:

_____ Check appearance in mirrors and/or shiny surfaces

_____ Avoid mirrors and/or shiny surfaces

_____ Use makeup excessively

_____ Use hats or clothing to hide or change the appearance of the body part of concern

_____ Use skin or hair products excessively

_____ Clean, peel, bleach skin

_____ Remove hair on face or other body parts

_____ Get frequent haircuts or hair treatments

_____ Groom, comb, smooth, straighten, or style hair excessively

_____ Exercise excessively

_____ Alter diet—eat too many or too few calories or avoid certain foods

_____ Engage in do-it-yourself surgery (attempt to change the perceived flaw in a manner that causes harm or damage to the body part)

_____ Squeeze, pinch, or stretch body parts to change their shape or form

_____ Research cosmetic or dermatological procedures

_____ Seek cosmetic or dermatological procedures

_____ Ask others for reassurance about your appearance

_____ Engage in skin picking

_____ Check body part by repeatedly touching or measuring body part of concern

_____ Compare yourself with others, such as strangers, friends, family, or celebrities

_____ Compare yourself with old photos of yourself

_____ Take photos of yourself excessively to assess how you look in different lights, positions, and so on

_____ Engage in facial exercises

_____ Avoid social contact (parties, dating, and so on)

_____ Avoid attendance of school or work

_____ Avoid situations involving potential scrutiny or attention (job interviews, bars/clubs)

_____ Avoid situations with perceived "competition" or emphasis on appearance—for example, others judged to be more "attractive" (bars/clubs, parties, and so on)

_____ Avoid crowded places

_____ Avoid brightly lit indoor places

_____ Avoid bright sunny days

_____ Sit in the back of a classroom or any other place so others do not notice you

_____ Other _____

We hope filling out this checklist has made you aware of all the ways in which BDD can interfere with your daily life. We'll refer back to this checklist in the treatment sections of this book, but for now, we encourage you to pay more attention to these behaviors.

It's true that most people want to look their best. However, the desire to look good exists on a continuum. That is, there are people who may not care or invest much thought or time in their looks, while others are obsessed with their appearance. People who are overly preoccupied with their appearance—be it shape, weight, or overall appearance—are said to have "body image disturbances," such as eating disorders or BDD. But since there's a continuum of this desire to look good, what exactly is "normal discontent"?

What Is Normal Discontent?

While some people are satisfied with the way they look and others are completely dissatisfied with their appearance, another large group falls in the middle. In the 1980s, Judith Rodin and colleagues (1984) created the term *normative discontent* to explain the widespread negative body feelings and attitudes of girls and women in Western cultures. (For our purposes, we'll call this "normal discontent.") While this was initially thought to affect women only, many men experience normal discontent as well. Many people suffer with normal discontent and have difficulties with their appearance without having BDD. Like those with BDD, they often shy away from expressing their concerns for fear of being perceived as conceited or vain.

How Does Normal Discontent Differ from BDD?

You may be saying to yourself, *I probably have normal discontent. After all, I'm one of those people who takes pride in taking care of myself.* Before you come to any conclusion, please read on and see what criteria fit you. In general, the concerns and apprehensions that people with BDD experience mirror the concerns and apprehensions of everyone else. So how can we tell the difference between normal discontent and BDD?

As we mentioned above, the critical differences between normal discontent and BDD are preoccupation with the perceived flaw and how much that preoccupation interferes with life and day-to-day functioning. This "flaw" can vary greatly: it can be an imagined flaw, a minor flaw, or a desire for a feature to be perfect. For example, people may say they look normal, but they really want to look extraordinary; for them, the flaw is not looking perfect. Whatever variety of "flaw" it is, all people with BDD share some type of preoccupation with what they perceive as their flaw, and that preoccupation interferes with life.

For you to have BDD, you need to think of the body part with which you are dissatisfied for at least one hour a day. We say "at least" because most people with BDD spend more than one hour. Actually, some spend countless hours thinking about their flaw.

Sometimes people with BDD seem as if they're not excessively preoccupied because they avoid trigger situations or camouflage the feature in such a way that their preoccupation isn't evident to others. However, if they weren't camouflaged or if they were put in a situation that they weren't prepared to be in, they would probably become anxious, uncomfortable, or upset.

When getting ready, people usually only devote a few minutes to checking out their appearance and do not tend to check for specific flaws or to see how their looks change with lighting, for instance. When choosing an outfit, most people make a choice and stick to it. So, if you're not certain what is normal, just ask a few people. We're sure that your friends and family would happily answer questions if you picked their brains about how they get ready.

If, however, you spend large amounts of time getting ready or making sure you're hiding a body part with which you are dissatisfied, you most likely have BDD. Pay attention to how many hours a day you spend on grooming and how you feel. If you spend a lot of energy and time and find yourself feeling unhappy, frustrated, or disgusted, then you probably have BDD.

"How do I look?" Just about everybody has uttered this phrase. While it's common for people to ask that of a close friend or family member every so often, do you ask that question over and over again? If so, you probably have BDD. Remember Keith, who is very concerned with hair loss and muscle mass? He often checks to see how his hairline changes throughout the day and during different activities, such as when he works out.

Keith often asks his parents if his hairline is receding further and how he should style his hair. His mother gets frustrated because she doesn't notice any hair loss. No matter what she says, Keith gets upset with her response. Sometimes she's so desperate to end the questioning that she asks him what exactly she should say to make him feel better. Like Keith, others with BDD often don't like the responses that they hear, and the people they ask may describe them as never seeming satisfied with an answer. Does that sound like you?

Remember, we all have a mental image of our body. We all think we know how we look. Sometimes we're surprised when we look at a photograph or a video and we can't believe that we look like that; it's not the way we imagined ourselves to be. It doesn't match our mental image. Well, you probably have a negative mental image of yourself, while individuals without BDD tend to have "rose-tinted glasses." Most often they perceive themselves to look better than others perceive them. In chapters 5 and 7, we'll help you learn how to change your negative mental image of the way you look.

Severity

A client once told us, "I don't have BDD because I'm not doing as badly as the people that I've read about." And that was true. Jenny had suffered with BDD for several years, but she was able to function fairly normally—at least until recently. Here's her story:

• Jenny: Mild BDD

Jenny was a stellar athlete and scholar and was very active in several extracurricular activities at her high school. She did everything that other high school seniors would do—attended the prom, hung out with friends, and so on. But there were little things that were different. While she had accounts on social networking websites, she would never post pictures, and she didn't even own a camera. She would wear makeup and keep up with fashion trends, but, for a night out with friends, she'd always find a way to get ready alone. Jenny was concerned with the bump on her nose. She worried about her upcoming transition to college and if her "ugly nose" would keep her from making friends. Despite her apprehension, she'd never talk about this for fear of being seen as "too into herself."

You may be like Jenny and feel that the cases that you have read about are more severe than anything that you deal with. There may be a few reasons for this. Perhaps the sites or articles that you read about BDD only addressed the more severe cases because they're the "most interesting." Or maybe you remember the more severe cases because they're unique and more likely to stick in your mind. While they have their similarities, people with BDD are like snowflakes: no two are alike in terms of concerns, symptoms, and severity. To see more examples of this range of severity, let's look at the cases of George (mild BDD), Yazmin (moderate BDD), and Harry (severe BDD).

• George: Mild BDD

George is a forty-five-year-old accountant who has his own firm. He has had BDD since he was sixteen, at which time he became obsessed with his moles. Like his father, he has a few moles on his body. George was a good high school student and went on to a good university. He hid his moles by wearing long sleeves, immediately putting on a cover after swimming, and using concealer. At times, he forgot about them; at other times, especially when he was anxious about exams, he was more bothered by them. George dated little, but during a good period he met Jane, a very understanding fine arts major. He ended up marrying her and having two children.

Over the years, he found that he didn't need to go swimming or do many outdoor sports that required revealing his arms. However, he does check them every night and asks Jane to do the same; he also checks them in his office. If for some reason he needs to bare his arms, such as during a physical, he uses concealer or only shows parts of his arms that don't have a mole. George leads a pretty average life, but he wishes his moles didn't interfere with his life at all.

• Yazmin: Moderate BDD

Yazmin is a twenty-three-year-old college student who believes she has blemishes that make her very unattractive. She also despises her curly hair and droopy eyes. A few years ago, she began college at an out-of-town university. As her first semester progressed, she attended classes less and less, and she found it very difficult to go to the cafeteria or to socialize in the dorm. One day, after her first semester, she had to return home. She broke down and told her parents she couldn't continue to go to school there. They picked her up and took her to a psychologist. Because Yazmin didn't initially reveal her real concerns (her appearance), her parents and psychologist thought she had social phobia and depression. Yazmin thought if she spoke about her appearance, everyone would think she was vain, which, of course, was far from the truth. She felt bad about her looks and could not run away from herself.

After a year of no progress, her parents decided she should try another therapist and brought her to us. As we do during all initial interviews, we asked her how she felt about her appearance. She looked so surprised and relieved that she told us the truth. Yazmin had been using foundations, concealers, and powder to hide what she perceived as noticeable blemishes, although they weren't visible to anyone else. She spent at least an hour a day straightening her hair and trying various products to get her hair to look perfect. She had tried all kinds of products to brighten the skin underneath her eyes. When she returned to her hometown—where she knew most of the people and was liked and accepted—she felt better and less stressed. She didn't think as much about her looks and spent drastically less time, money, and effort on getting ready. She was able to head back to school again and is now taking one or two courses a semester at a community college. To help her do this, she initially engaged in intensive therapy, which helped her expose herself to situations she feared while not camouflaging her flaws.

• Harry: Severe BDD

Harry is thirty-five years old and lives with his parents and twenty-four-year-old brother. He has a long history of struggling with BDD. Although he had inklings of it during his senior year in high school, it didn't get really bad until he was completing his senior year in college. He managed to complete a premed program by studying long hours on his own, taking night classes, and having his own private apartment so he didn't need to socialize. By his senior year, he was worn out but kept plugging along. He'd been concerned about his hairline and nose, and he believed that others were talking about him and laughing behind his back. He didn't date and justified it by saying that he was committed to doing well and getting into medical school. During his holidays at home, he slept most of the time and kept to himself. His family attributed this behavior to his long and arduous hours at school.

By the time he had applied to medical school and gotten in, Harry had to take a one-year leave of absence. He could no longer avoid classes and couldn't interact with professors and other medical students. Eventually, his long hours of preoccupation about his hair, constant mirror checking, hours fussing with his hair and holding his hand over his nose didn't allow him to return to medical school. He became suicidal, knowing he wasn't going to complete his degree and lifelong dream. He was hospitalized for depression and eventually ended up being homebound. However, he experienced no peace there because his younger brother, who had moved home after college to save money, would bring friends home. This bothered Harry tremendously, and he and his brother would end up fighting. His parents told him he either had to get help or move into a halfway house. He chose to come for help.

As you can see, BDD severity can range from relatively mild to very severe. Some people, like Jenny and George, seem to function normally; others, like Yazmin, struggle, but with assistance, they can cope fairly well; still others, like Harry, are so severely compromised in their lives that they really struggle every day and are unable to do those things that are most important to them. Despite this range in severity, it's important to keep in mind that all people with BDD do have things in common. Can you guess what those are, based on the reading that you have done so far? If you said preoccupation and interference with life, then you're right.

EXERCISE: With Whom Do You Identify?

While reading the stories above, you probably thought about which of these folks you're most like. If you haven't, then do it now! With whom do you most relate when it comes to symptom severity? Is it Jenny, George,

Yazmin, or Harry? Jot down the name and his or her corresponding severity level in your notebook. We'll come back to this in a later chapter.

What happens if you have moderate to severe BDD? You may feel that your options in life are very limited. You may leave school, quit your job, become homebound, avoid obligations and responsibilities, abuse alcohol and/or drugs, become hospitalized, attempt do-it-yourself surgery, and think about or attempt suicide.

SUICIDALITY AND BDD

As you can see, severe BDD can cause very debilitating effects. Sufferers sometimes experience such extreme pain and torment that they think that the only way to end such hurt would be to kill themselves. Thinking about suicide is quite common among those who suffer from BDD. Almost 80 percent have thoughts about ending their lives. A relatively sizable amount, about 20 percent, attempt it, but thankfully few succeed.

• Oliver's Story

Oliver had suffered with BDD for quite some time. He really didn't have a particular flaw that he was concerned with but felt that he was ugly overall. He felt that he was so unattractive that no one would ever want to be with him. He watched his friends date seriously, get engaged and married, and settle down to start a family. That was all that he wanted. Oliver made the decision that, despite his symptoms, he was going to put himself out in the dating scene.

One night, he went out with friends; their last stop was a diner. As his friends recounted the night, Oliver was focused on the waitress. He found her attractive and wanted to "test" his attractiveness by seeing how she would react to him. She came over and took their order, as she did with every other table. Oliver became extremely upset because "she looked longer at everyone else at the table. She thought I was hideous." At that moment, Oliver made the decision to end his life that night: "If a waitress couldn't even look at me, how can

I ever get married or have children?" On his way out, he called his brother to tell him his plan and hung up the phone.

Oliver drove and drove until he found a desolate bridge. He stood out there for hours, replaying the scenario, thinking about everything he'd missed out on in life. He became scared and called his therapist, saying he was uncertain of what to do. Oliver decided to return home. He checked himself into the hospital and continued with his treatment, though he was skeptical about ever feeling better. With the right treatment, Oliver was successful. He is now married, with a child on the way.

As you can see from Oliver's story, it's possible to move beyond suicide, even when you feel you've hit rock bottom. We know that reaching out for help when you don't believe anything will work is very hard or embarrassing, but if you're experiencing suicidal thoughts, have had images of dying, or have imagined or made plans on how you would end your life, we urge you to tell someone immediately. Find a friend or relative you trust, call your family physician, reach out to your guidance counselor or social worker at school, or, if you're currently in treatment, call your therapist or psychiatrist. If these thoughts and urges are really intense and you feel you're going to act on them now or very soon, the safest place to seek help is your local emergency room.

Levels of Insight

You may hear someone say, "She has no insight into her problems. She has gotten so bad that she hardly wants to do anything." Contrary to popular belief, *insight*, or, in the case of BDD, the ability to know that your problems come from BDD and are not totally realistic, isn't related to how severe your symptoms are. People with BDD can vary in terms of insight— having good insight to poor or no insight at all. Some people have very mild symptoms and no insight, while others have very severe symptoms and good insight. If you have good insight, you realize that the way you perceive your appearance is inaccurate. If you have poor insight, you're convinced that the way you perceive yourself is completely accurate, even when others don't agree with you—that is, you can't see the symptoms as irrational or extreme, and you truly believe that your concerns are real and the behaviors you engage in are helpful.

Some people, in addition to having BDD, fit into criteria for what is called a "delusional disorder, somatic type." When people are *delusional*, they're resolute in their belief that their perceived flaw does exist, despite statements from others and evidence to the contrary. They have poor or no insight into their beliefs about their appearance. Approximately 36 percent of people with BDD also meet criteria for a delusional disorder at some point in their life. Don't be discouraged if you think you fit these criteria, because you can respond to treatment too.

Insight is one aspect of evaluating how you view your beliefs about your body part of concern. There are other related variables, such as how reasonable, how accurate, and how strongly you are convinced that your thoughts are true. Fugen Neziroglu and her colleagues (1999) developed a scale called the Overvalued Ideas Scale to precisely assess insight and many other factors. You can find this scale in chapter 5.

We've been discussing the difference between normal discontent and BDD. The exercise below will help you understand if your symptoms are more consistent with normal discontent or with BDD.

EXERCISE: Normal Discontent vs. BDD

Read over the following list and check the items that you agree with.

_____ 1. I can continue with my day even if I'm not completely satisfied with my appearance.

_____ 2. I focus excessively on myself and give a lot of attention to particular features.

_____ 3. I spend excessive time getting ready only for special occasions or when necessary (for example, weddings, job interviews, first dates).

_____ 4. I spend over one hour per day thinking or doing something about my appearance.

_____ 5. Frustrations with appearance don't get in the way of my day-to-day functioning.

_____ 6. I won't go out or be seen by others unless my appearance is just so.

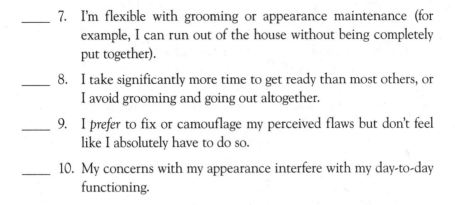

_____ 7. I'm flexible with grooming or appearance maintenance (for example, I can run out of the house without being completely put together).

_____ 8. I take significantly more time to get ready than most others, or I avoid grooming and going out altogether.

_____ 9. I *prefer* to fix or camouflage my perceived flaws but don't feel like I absolutely have to do so.

_____ 10. My concerns with my appearance interfere with my day-to-day functioning.

If you checked off more of the odd-numbered items, then your body image concerns are more in line with normal discontent. The even-numbered items are symptoms of BDD. Because these items fall on a continuum, it's possible that people with BDD can also check items that people with normal discontent would check.

For those of you who are very preoccupied, spend time engaging in the various behaviors we listed above, may at times become suicidal, and are pretty sure others would think you have poor insight, you probably suffer from BDD and not normal discontent.

Types of BDD Symptoms

BDD symptoms can be broken down into three different categories: behaviors (how we act), thoughts (how we think, our ideas), and emotions (how we feel). Let's take a closer look at each of these categories.

Behaviors

Depending on how preoccupied you are with your appearance, you'll attempt to reduce your discomfort and your preoccupation by engaging in a variety of behaviors. BDD behaviors are pesky to maintain, and they interfere with everyday life. Just planning them out—for example, "Where am I going to sit in the restaurant to avoid bad lighting?"—is taxing and requires a lot of energy. These behaviors interfere with life goals, with fun, and with building and maintaining friendships and other relationships. As much as these behaviors may seem to help you, they actually are *countertherapeutic*—that is, they get in the way of your symptoms improving. Let's say that Kelly decided not to go to college because she fears that she's so ugly that nobody would want to befriend her. Then, because she's so upset about this decision, she spends her days in her bedroom, isolating herself from her family and friends. With Kelly spending all of her time in her room, she'll never be able to prove her BDD wrong by being able to go out and make friends. If anything, staying in her bedroom adds a more convincing argument that her BDD thoughts are right, because she won't make new friends confined to her bedroom! As you can see, such behaviors can make BDD worse and increase other symptoms, such as depression, low self-esteem, and lack of self-confidence.

Now let's review common types of BDD behaviors.

COMMON BDD BEHAVIORS

Mirror avoidance. Clients are often confused as to whether using the mirror or avoiding the mirror is symptomatic of their BDD. You actually may engage in one or the other, or alternate between behaviors. Mirror avoidance is usually used to prevent lengthy mirror checking or avoid BDD thoughts and feelings. It's not the same as using the mirror functionally and resisting the urge to check. Thirty percent of people with BDD avoid mirrors, while 67 percent selectively avoid mirrors—that is, they avoid some mirrors that they feel aren't particularly flattering (Phillips et al. 1997).

Here are the types of selective avoidance:

- Avoiding looking at the perceived flaw

- Avoiding certain mirrors (those labeled as "good" or "bad"—mirrors in certain rooms may be "better" than others due to lighting or positioning)

- Avoiding use of mirrors in public

Mirror checking and other checking behaviors. As mentioned in the introduction, mirror checking is a behavior used by an overwhelming majority of people with BDD. When mirror checking, your focus is more likely on the specific body parts and features perceived as flawed rather than your whole body or your whole face. While you may use various mirrors or just stick to one that you believe tells the "truth" or is the most flattering, you may also use reflective surfaces that don't give a clear reflection, such as kitchen appliances, CDs, or store windows. When we refer to mirror checking, we're also including any reflective surface. Mirror checking serves multiple purposes:

- To know how you look in that moment

- To hide flaws

- To improve appearance

- To see if something has changed or become different

- To compare yourself to the image that you have in your mind

You may also gaze because you wish to look different or because you do not trust your memory of your last mirror check. Mirror checking may involve going from one mirror to another to confirm what you saw in the other mirror.

While you may have good intentions for mirror checking, you're likely to feel depressed when doing so. Mirror checking then exacerbates these negative feelings, which continue to increase after you leave the mirror.

Using reflective surfaces isn't the only way to validate your appearance. Looking at and taking photographs is a common way to verify appearance. Digital cameras and cellular phones equipped with cameras make it quite easy to check your appearance anywhere. One of our clients was so convinced that the lighting in her car made her look strange that she checked this by taking pictures while driving. Digital cameras can hold thousands of photos, and it's easy to erase them and keep them from others. Photos can also be used for comparison—for example, comparing current appearance to an old photo. You may look to the past because then you perceived your appearance as better, or you may look at previous photos to confirm that the flaw was always there.

While you can use a reflective surface or a camera to check physical flaws, you can also use your internal picture of yourself, which is not likely to be the most dependable source. Or you can touch or look at the flaw that isn't on your face. You can also push or squeeze body parts, do "exercises" to change them, and measure them.

Comparing your flaw to the features of others is yet another common BDD behavior. You may compare your flaw to people you know well or to people you see elsewhere: magazines, television, social networking sites, and other media outlets. Usually the perceived flaw is compared to that same feature on those of the same sex. So, if you're a woman, you likely use other women as your comparison points; men usually compare themselves to other men. For example, during his lunch break, Ben would often sit in a crowded city park in order to compare himself to other men as they passed by. Sometimes he would become so overwhelmed with this process and feeling the need to look at every man near his age who walked by that he would follow them to ensure that he had looked at them correctly. He felt very anxious that one of these men would notice him staring or following him, but he felt compelled to do so anyway. Though it's most common for women to compare themselves to women and for men to compare themselves to men, some people compare themselves with the opposite sex. Comparing skin tone and complexion are common examples.

Cosmetic and dermatological procedures. Cosmetic and dermatological procedures are safety-seeking behaviors to prevent feeling bad about the way you look. You may believe these procedures will change your appearance permanently or restore it to what it looked like in the past; you might seek, for example, a face-lift or Botox injections to re-create a more youthful appearance. Other possibilities include cosmetic surgery (liposuction), dermatological procedures (laser resurfacing), hair transplants, and dental work. On the more extreme end, some may consider do-it-yourself surgery, where they act as the surgeon and try to change their own appearance. In addition to undergoing such procedures, you may spend inordinate amounts of time researching various procedures online, trying the latest products and fads, and consulting with surgeons and dermatologists. You may fantasize endlessly about how you'll look after having a procedure, which is known as mental cosmetic surgery. However, if you do have a procedure done, you may feel that the results aren't as you expected and you may then seek out more procedures to further enhance your appearance.

Makeup and skin behaviors. It's quite common for people, especially women, to use makeup to enhance their appearance. You may use makeup excessively to hide your flaws. This can lead to further mirror checking to retouch and make certain that the makeup does its job. While makeup use is more commonly associated with women, men with BDD may also use makeup to conceal flaws or to hide blemishes, moles, or other perceived problems.

While you may avoid makeup products, you may be preoccupied with your skin being scrupulously clean. This can lead to excessive use of cleansers, peels, and facials. You may be very cautious about sun exposure, trying to avoid it as much as possible and/or being invested in finding the best and most effective sunscreen. To cleanse the skin, you may also pick your skin's blemishes. If you're a man, you may shave excessively or avoid shaving in order to protect your skin. And rather than avoiding sun exposure, you may be tanning to camouflage your flaws. Many of our clients use tanning salons for the sole purpose of camouflaging, hiding their flaws, or making their skin look more attractive.

Hair as camouflage. Hair is so important for most people. The expression "It is a good- (or bad-) hair day" really says it all. No matter who or what the concern, hair plays a very important role in how people feel about themselves. In BDD, hair can play a pivotal role. Several BDD behaviors involve the hair: combing/brushing/styling, receiving hair treatments (like deep conditionings and Brazilian hair straightening), cutting hair, and using various products or different types of hairstyling appliances. Hair can also be used in lots of ways to camouflage. You may wear your hair hanging down around the face to hide your facial flaws. If you're concerned with losing your hair, you may be overly focused on hair-loss treatments, or you may camouflage by wearing a hat. You may have trouble having your hair cut or styled in a salon for fear of scrutiny by the cosmetician. You may choose to cut your own hair, believing that you can get the "just right" length. Concern over your hair may lead to pulling your hair, or coloring it often and being dissatisfied, or you may be so desperate after many attempts to get your hair just right that you decide to wear a wig to hide your flaw or cover your mistakes in attempting to camouflage it. We're not suggesting that if you get your hair straightened, color your hair, or put mousse in your hair, you have BDD. Whether or not you have BDD depends on how much time you spend, how distressed you are, and whether your preoccupation with your hair affects your daily living.

Hiding behind clothes. Just as hats may be used to camouflage, clothing also may be used to hide flaws. You may use clothes to hide your flaws or reduce your eye contact with other people. You can use loose-fitting clothing to hide your shape or layer up to enlarge areas of your body, such as the breasts, or to bulk up if you feel that you're too thin. For example, due to relentless teasing during his early teen years, Curtis always wore no less than three shirts in order to appear bigger. Summer always frustrated him because he couldn't layer. However, every season can be grueling if you spend inordinate amounts of time preparing and trying on outfits before leaving the house. Sandra complained that she lacked time to devote to her homework and exercising, so she would fast and undertake fad diets. With Sandra, we examined her day and found that she would spend over an hour every night preparing her outfit for the following day. And at times she would still feel frustrated in the morning before school and spend an extra thirty minutes getting her outfit right to hide her "hideous thighs."

Using body posturing, hands, and other props. Other ways to camouflage include how you hold yourself. You may be hypervigilant about how you hold and tilt your head, or you may avoid being seen in profile or from whatever angle you feel is unflattering or exposes your flaws. You may place your hands carefully in order to hide your perceived flaw, or you may sit or stand in a certain way to minimize the shape of your thighs. There are endless ways that body posturing can be used to camouflage or minimize flaws. Additionally, you may use objects or props, such as an oversized purse, sunglasses, or books, to hide your features.

Reassurance seeking. Reassurance seeking is used when you feel uncertain about your appearance. It consists of asking others to confirm the flaw—that is, you usually want to convince people that the flaw truly does exist. You may become very angry or frustrated with the response you receive. The people you ask are likely to feel angry and frustrated too, because they feel you don't accept their answer. On one hand, you may feel upset because you think they're lying if they don't confirm the flaw or because you feel that they can never give you the right answer. On the other hand, you may seek reassurance to confirm that the strategies you used to "look better" really worked and/or that you're truly not as flawed as you feel. Even if you use reassurance seeking for these purposes, you'll most likely be disappointed anyway. You'll probably still feel that people try to make you feel better or that they don't see the flaw because you're so dear to them. In other words, you discount what they say and continue to feel miserable.

GENERAL AVOIDANCE

Avoidance comes in a variety of forms: avoiding social situations, activities in public, or dating and sexual intimacy; wearing unflattering clothing; dodging the camera and social networking sites; and avoiding mirrors or places that may highlight the feature or flaw. The list goes on and on.

EXERCISE: Which Behaviors Do You Engage In?

Now it's time to pull out that handy notebook and pen. Follow these steps:

1. Write down some of the behaviors you engage in to decrease, prevent, or escape from your uncomfortable feelings. Try to think of all of them. You may engage in some of the behaviors listed above, so check those out; be sure to add any that aren't listed.

2. How many behaviors have you listed?

3. Were you aware of them prior to listing them?

4. How will identifying the behaviors help you stop them later on?

Thoughts

Are you preoccupied with troubling thoughts about your particular body part? Are you even more preoccupied with how others view you? These bothersome thoughts cause a lot of frustration. They're like boomerangs—you try to throw them away, but they just come back. These troubling thoughts are symptoms of BDD.

We find that some people just want to blend in, while others want to be noticed. In other words, some believe they're below average and want to be "normal," and others think they're "okay" but want to be above average. Here are some common thoughts:

- *People are taking special notice of my flaw.*

- *Appearance is everything.*

- *People only judge others by their appearance.*

- *I can't do anything until I feel that I look just right.*

- *All I care about is blending in with others so I won't be stared at.*

- *If celebrities can be really beautiful, why can't I?*

- *My nose has a bump on it.*

- *My hair texture is awful.*

- *My facial features aren't symmetrical.*

- *My hips aren't smooth.*

- *I hate my skin. It's not as clear as everybody else's skin.*

- *My clitoris is too long.*

- *I'm just ugly overall. I can't tell just one thing because it's just everything.*

- *I have a weak chin.*

- *My hairline is receding.*

- *I'm too hairy! I look like the Wolfman!*

- *My cheeks still have baby fat.*

- *My ears stick out too much.*

- *My teeth aren't white enough.*

- *I'm too skinny.*

Start paying attention to your thoughts. Write them down over the next couple of days. We'll refer to them in future chapters. If you can't identify any, we'll help you do that in later chapters; we'll also teach you how to think a little differently.

Emotions

You probably experience a whole host of emotions as part of your BDD. The most common are listed below. Above we asked you to write down the thoughts that you have. In the next few days, when you have a thought, pay attention to what you're feeling as you have that thought. Write your feelings next to your thoughts.

DEPRESSION

Probably the most common emotion in BDD is depression. How often during the week do you feel sad, feel that nothing will change in your life, or feel that you are doomed to live a horrible existence because of your appearance? Depression may be a direct result of feeling bad about your appearance and not being able to change it. How do you feel when you aren't able to do the things you would like in your life because of your BDD? How about when you try to change your appearance and you can't, such as when you still feel "ugly" despite camouflaging or excessive groom-ing, or when the dermatological products don't seem to help? Remember Matthew, whom you met in the introduction? Matthew felt depressed after being turned down for cosmetic surgery. Some individuals become more depressed after they pursue surgery and do not get the results they seek. Sometimes people can feel sad, tearful, or blue. It can last for hours or it can last for weeks, months, or even years. There's a difference between being sad and having clinical depression, which is known as "major depres-sive disorder." We'll discuss major depressive disorder later in this chapter.

ANXIETY

Depression and anxiety go hand in hand. Anxiety can manifest as physical sensations and/or how you feel. If you're about to go out, meet someone, go to work, go to school, go on a date, or get lunch/dinner, do you feel anxious? Do you begin to experience restlessness or jitteriness? Does your heart race? Do you feel nauseated all of a sudden? You may have sweaty hands, feel dizzy, have wobbly knees, experience a knot in your stomach, or feel out of it. These are all physical symptoms of anxiety. Even if you don't have any physical symptoms you can *feel* anxious. How do you experience anxiety? When do you feel anxiety? Is it when you go out of your comfort zone, when you check the mirror, when you see others, or when you compare yourself to people in magazines or on TV? Do you feel anxious when you compare yourself to people in general?

SHAME

In psychology, we rarely speak of shame, a common emotion for all of us in many different types of situations. When Ana thought others were noticing her complexion, she felt ashamed. We call this *external shame*— when there are thoughts and feelings about being inferior, defective, ugly, or bad. You believe that others look at you and condemn you for failing to achieve an external standard or for having an unappealing appearance. The emphasis is on another person's negative evaluation or scrutiny of the flawed body part. Body shame is quite common for all individuals suffering with BDD. Not all individuals with BDD have external shame, however. Many have *internal shame*, in which one views oneself as being inferior, defective, ugly, and a failure to achieve an internal standard of beauty. In other words, there's a discrepancy between one's actual and ideal self. Internal shame is associated with perfectionism, or the relentless pursuit of a perfect or ideal self.

DISGUST

Disgust is a basic emotion that's an aversion to something or someone that's repulsive or offensive. Disgust reactions are distinctly different from anxiety. Words that are often associated with disgust include "icky," "gross," "nasty," and "yuck." Think of feces, blood, seeing an animal being eaten by another animal, or viewing someone perform surgery. What kind of reaction do you have to those images? Do you cringe and wrinkle your nose? You may usually think that disgust refers to not eating something because you find it repulsive, but that same sense of repulsion can apply to your appearance. In one study of ours, we found that our BDD clients had higher disgust sensitivity than other individuals (Neziroglu, Hickey, and McKay 2010). Do you say things like these?

- "My (complexion, nose, or hair) is disgusting."

- "I can't go out looking so hideous and disgusting."

- "I hate the way my _____ (fill in the blank) looks; it's just disgusting."

- "People are disgusted when they see my profile, and I don't blame them."

- "How could anyone want to date me when I'm so disgusting?"

- "I wouldn't go out with me."

See how often you think of yourself or think others think of you as disgusting.

ANGER

Anger is a common emotion in BDD. You may be angry for a variety of reasons. It's often a *secondary emotion*. That means that sometimes you feel angry as a result of feeling other emotions like depression, anxiety, shame, embarrassment, and disgust. Here are other reasons for feeling angry:

- Being misunderstood by others

- Feeling frustrated for not being able to change your appearance to your liking

- Being teased

- Being laughed at

- Being ignored

- Having to deal with things that are difficult for you but apparently easy for others

- Not looking like people you admire

- Being told you're attractive when you think you aren't

Anger usually occurs when one is hurt. It can be directed toward oneself or others. In chapter 10, we'll address managing your anger toward your friends and family.

Now that you've learned about the emotions that are common in BDD, take note of your own emotions—that is, how you feel and under what circumstances you feel that way. Remember that you can feel more than one emotion at a time. In later chapters, you'll learn how to manage these emotions.

Subtypes of BDD

Now that we have explained the general BDD behaviors, thoughts, and emotions, let's look closer at some specific subtypes of BDD. BDD can focus on any bodily part or feature; however, the following subtypes and related disorders have prompted their own distinct names and research.

Skin Picking

Skin picking is a behavior used to enhance appearance in BDD by removing a blemish or something that someone perceives as unattractive. Skin picking can consist of picking, scratching, digging, rubbing, and/or squeezing of normal skin or skin with minimal blemishes. It usually involves acne, scars, "large" pores, blackheads, whiteheads, bumps, "ugly things," or some attempt to remove impurities in the skin. The behavior may take on a life of its own, but the motivation behind it is to enhance appearance. Of course, one does not need to have BDD to engage in skin picking. There are people who do not have BDD and whose skin picking does not serve to enhance their image.

Koro: Panic over Penis Shrinking

Koro, or genital retraction syndrome, is a man's fear that his penis will shrink or withdraw into the body and cause death. This can be seen in women as well, but then, of course, it refers to other body parts, namely the breasts and/or labia. Koro has been explained as a different form of BDD that occurs in other cultures, primarily in Asia. The difference between BDD and koro is that koro is usually marked by fleeting, acute anxiety and avoidance, and family members also believe that body part will retract, leading to death. Family members often attempt to help keep the body part from retracting and do things like pull it or place a clamp on it. While men with BDD may have thoughts that their penises are too small or are shrinking, most don't share the belief of koro sufferers that this will result in death or that their penis is retracting and will disappear.

Muscle Dysmorphia: Obsession with Muscle Size

Often described as the reverse form of anorexia nervosa, *muscle dysmorphia* is the fear of and excessive preoccupation with being small, frail, and weak. People with anorexia fear being fat, so they engage in behaviors like excessive dieting. In contrast to people with anorexia, people with muscle dysmorphia engage in behaviors—exercising excessively, abusing steroids, taking supplements, and drinking protein shakes—because they fear being too thin. They may also camouflage themselves with clothing or pad themselves to cover up thin areas.

Olfactory Reference Syndrome (ORS): Obsession with One's Body Odor

Olfactory reference syndrome (ORS) is a preoccupation with body odor and/or bad breath. A great sense of shame usually accompanies the perceived odor. People with ORS may experience hallucinations where they perceive that they actually smell a foul odor being emitted. Like BDD, ORS has safety behaviors in order to cover the perceived unpleasant odor. These include wearing excessive perfume/cologne, constantly reapplying deodorant, putting soap or potpourri sacks near their genitalia, showering frequently, changing clothing often, brushing teeth, chewing gum, and eating mints. In addition to masking with safety behaviors, people with ORS may also avoid situations, such as going to the gym, where they feel that others may notice their body odor. They usually try to stay far away from others.

BDD by Proxy: Obsession with Flaws in Others

BDD by proxy is an excessive preoccupation with the imagined flaws of another person. Individuals with this disorder may or may not worry about their own appearance. Sometimes it's the same area of concern— that is, someone with BDD who is preoccupied with the shape of his lips may become preoccupied with another person's lips. BDD by proxy interferes often with the individual's ability to date or have friends. The minute people with BDD by proxy notice a flaw in another person, they feel disgusted and aren't able to be around that individual. We have seen individuals who had to withdraw from classes because they couldn't look at a teacher who had a minor flaw.

Conditions Related to BDD

Now that you have a better idea of what BDD is, let's look at disorders that are related. You may be wondering why we address other disorders when you're interested in learning about BDD, right? Although someone may suffer from only BDD, it's not uncommon for people to have co-occurring conditions as well. The likelihood of someone with BDD having another disorder is quite high. The most common co-occurring disorders are major depressive disorder, social phobia, and obsessive-compulsive disorder. When treating BDD, it's important to also address any other ongoing issues.

Major Depressive Disorder

Many people use the term "depressed" to mean that they feel sad or to express that they're having a bad day. Clinical depression, or major depressive disorder, however, is more serious than having a temporary case of the blues.

When we become depressed, we're inclined to do less and less. Our motivation and interest in life deteriorates. Things that were once pleasurable are no longer pleasurable. We sleep more or experience insomnia. We eat more or less. It becomes harder to concentrate.

All of these symptoms are so overwhelming that they can lead to shrugging off our day-to-day tasks and responsibilities. We start to procrastinate and avoid. It becomes less important to tend to chores, go to the gym, or even do the fun things in life like spend time with loved ones or watch a movie. As time goes on, the list of things that we have to do builds and builds, which can lead to more avoidance and more negative feelings—worthlessness, hopelessness, guilt, and further depression. Sometimes we become so depressed that we start having thoughts about suicide, and some people act on them.

The difference between depression and BDD is that the depressed mood goes beyond just appearance. Nonetheless, people with BDD have a high likelihood of experiencing depression at some point during their lives (Gunstad and Phillips 2003; Veale and Neziroglu 2010). Depressive symptoms usually develop after BDD. Sometimes people only present their depressive symptoms to treatment providers, out of shame or a need for secrecy. If you suffer with both BDD and depression without telling your treatment provider that you also have BDD, you won't be treated appropriately. If you're in treatment, please inform your mental health provider because both depression and BDD can be difficult to manage. If you have both BDD and depression, suicide is a greater risk, so your condition should be monitored closely.

Social Phobia

When people have *social phobia*, they believe that others are judging or evaluating them in some negative way. They are extremely self-conscious, believing that their behavior will in some way be unacceptable to others. They tend to concentrate on what others think about them in social situations rather than on the discussion or the event that is taking place. They feel embarrassed, humiliated, or anxious. Social phobia may include difficulty speaking in front of others, being on stage, eating with others, or writing or performing for others.

Both BDD sufferers and people with social phobia avoid social situations—in this way they are similar—but they differ in that people with social phobia think their *behavior and thoughts* will be judged negatively, while people with BDD think their *appearance* will be evaluated negatively. Both experience the same type of emotions but for different reasons. However, it's possible for people to have both social phobia and BDD, which means they would fear how they look and how they act. Social phobia is the second most frequently found co-occurring diagnosis after depression. Research has found that, unlike with depression, people with both social phobia and BDD tend to develop social phobia first (Veale and Neziroglu 2010).

Obsessive-Compulsive Disorder (OCD)

Obsessive-compulsive disorder (OCD) consists of obsessions and compulsions. *Obsessions* are recurring, unwanted, intrusive thoughts, images, or impulses that get stuck in one's head. Common obsessions are fears of contamination or of hurting oneself or others, desires for symmetry and perfection, and thoughts that are sexual or aggressive. *Compulsions* are physical actions or mental acts that one feels need to be completed to reduce anxiety, usually as a response to an obsession. Common compulsions are washing, checking, counting, ordering, and praying. OCD is similar to BDD in that both involve obsessions and compulsions; however, BDD thoughts and behaviors are appearance specific. Many BDD researchers consider BDD a kind of OCD.

Personality Disorders

Personality disorders consist of enduring patterns of behaviors and experiences that vary from what is expected in one's culture. Studies have shown many people with BDD have a personality disorder (Veale and Neziroglu 2010) and usually more than one type (Neziroglu et al. 1996). They found that the most common personality disorders present with BDD are avoidant, paranoid, obsessive-compulsive, dependent, and borderline personality disorders. We don't know if a personality disorder comes before BDD or if BDD causes personality to change. We do know that if someone has a personality disorder in addition to BDD, it's important to address these patterns so that they don't interfere with treatment.

Trichotillomania: Compulsive Hair Pulling

Trichotillomania is recurrent pulling of one's hair to the extent that it causes visible hair loss. Like other diagnoses, it also affects functioning. Hair can be pulled, creating bald spots, from many areas: eyelashes, eyebrows, scalp, pubic area, and other parts of the body. Reasons for pulling include reducing tension and gaining a sense of pleasure from pulling. Hair pulling can occur in BDD. Camouflaging and avoidant behaviors are common to both BDD and trichotillomania. The difference between them is that hair pulling in BDD is specific to appearance enhancement. In BDD, people pull their hair because they believe it's disgusting and that having skin without hair is appealing.

Eating Disorders

There are two major types of eating disorders: anorexia nervosa and bulimia nervosa. These conditions involve distorted body image, preoccupations with weight, and troubling eating patterns.

Anorexia nervosa is the refusal to maintain normal body weight and a fear of gaining weight despite being underweight. People with anorexia usually starve themselves. *Bulimia nervosa* consists of episodes of bingeing and purging. *Binge eating* is defined by consuming very large amounts of food in a relatively short period of time. Bingeing episodes are sometimes followed by purging, which includes self-induced vomiting or use of laxatives or diuretics, to compensate for any potential weight gain.

Eating disorders are associated with BDD because they involve body image disturbance and other symptoms, such as compulsive behaviors and perfectionism. Distinguishing between BDD and an eating disorder can be tricky. In order to be diagnosed with both BDD and an eating disorder, there must be disordered eating, concern related to being overweight or "too fat," and concern with another part of the body not related to weight. If the concern is solely on weight and disordered eating is present, then it may be categorized as an eating disorder only. However, our experience has shown that many eating disordered people are also preoccupied with many body parts. The two seem to go hand in hand. In other words, you may be preoccupied with your weight, think your stomach, buttocks, and thighs are fat (common in eating disorders), and, at the same time, think that your arms are too long and your complexion is red and ugly. In that case, you would have an eating disorder and BDD.

Substance Use and Abuse

In order to escape the pains that are common in BDD, some people abuse alcohol or other drugs, whether prescription or street drugs, in order to escape or avoid their BDD thoughts and/or behaviors. While it may seem helpful, the escape is short-lived and does not help treat the BDD. Substances, like alcohol and marijuana, can actually exacerbate a depressed mood and decrease motivation.

EXERCISE: Do You Suffer from Any Conditions Related to BDD?

Now that you have a better idea of symptoms of BDD, let's examine if you have any disorders that are often related to BDD. Only a licensed mental health professional can properly diagnose you. Here's a preliminary assessment, consisting of common symptoms of each disorder. If you answer yes to any of the following questions and they interfere with your life or make you feel anxious or stressed, you should consider seeking professional help.

Depression

1. a. Do you feel down or depressed most of the day almost every day?

1. b. Has there been a change in your sleeping habits recently?

1. c. Has there been a change in your appetite or in your weight recently?

1. d. Do you experience feelings of guilt or hopelessness?

1. e. Have you lost interest in activities that were previously pleasurable?

Social Phobia

2. a. Do you ever feel anxious, uncomfortable, or frightened doing things in front of other people (speaking, eating, making a speech, talking on the phone)?

2. b. Do you fear that you'll do or say something embarrassing in front of others or that they'll judge you negatively?

2. c. Do you avoid attending social situations because of your fear of being judged or concern about doing something embarrassing?

2. d. Do others consider you excessively shy?

Obsessive-Compulsive Disorder

3. a. Do you ever have bothersome thoughts or images that are really hard to get out of your head?

3. b. Do you ever feel like you need to do something that you cannot resist doing again and again (hand washing, praying, checking)?

3. c. Do you worry about harm coming to yourself or others?

3. d. Do you check things over and over again?

Trichotillomania

4. a. Do you repeatedly pull out your hair from your scalp, eyebrows, eyelashes, or another part of your body, resulting in hair loss?

4. b. Do you experience urges to pull out your hair and experience a sense of relief once you pull?

4. c. Do you have hair missing from parts of your scalp, your eyelashes, or other parts of your body?

Eating Disorders

5. a. Do you ever feel like your eating is out of control?

5. b. Do you weigh significantly less than others think you should weigh?

5. c. Do you ever eat a lot more in one sitting than other people? Do you ever eat a lot in secret?

5. d. Do you ever engage in any behaviors to make up for the fact that you thought you ate more than you should have (vomiting, taking laxatives, excessive exercising)?

Now you have learned about what BDD is and how it is manifested in people's lives. We focused on how body image disturbances go from normal discontent to extreme body image disorders. This may have led you to wonder what causes some people to go on to develop BDD while others do not. Let's explore that in the next chapter.

2

How Did You Get Body Dysmorphic Disorder?

So what causes BDD? You may have been asking yourself this question for some time now. Can you blame the way your parents disciplined you as a child? How about those terrible middle school years when you developed acne and your peers cruelly teased you? Unfortunately, while we can't give you a simple answer to your question, we can provide you with some clues. Researchers believe that people with BDD may have certain innate "biological" factors, which, combined with particular life experiences, lead to the disorder. Essentially, this is called the *biopsychosocial model*. Simply put, the model suggests that a combination of one's biological/genetic makeup, psychological influences, and environmental factors combine to affect the person's development of a particular condition. It's the most common psychological theory used to explain why humans develop any particular disorder.

In this chapter, we'll review the biopsychosocial influences in BDD development. As you read, you may notice that some of these risk factors are not unique to BDD. After all, lots of people can recall feeling humiliated, teased, or bullied at some time in childhood, but they didn't develop BDD. But as we said above, it's the combination of certain factors that influence the way in which the disorder develops.

Biological Influences

So how can science even assume that biology plays a role in the development of BDD? Can't we blame the appearance-focused society we live in? After all, we're all bombarded with images and media messages suggesting that beauty leads to wealth, love, respect, happiness, and overall success. Aren't most people influenced by these images on television and in magazines? Aren't most people dissatisfied with their bodies? The answer to both questions is yes, and in fact, research even supports this. But, as we established in the last chapter, there are distinct differences between normal discontent and BDD. Since we all live in similar cultures with similar influences, we can conclude that BDD can't simply be due to our sociocultural influences. Furthermore, some fascinating recent research supports the idea that BDD is partly a brain-based disorder (Feusner, Yaryura-Tobias, and Saxena 2008; Saxena and Feusner 2006). Let's start by reviewing the current medical knowledge about BDD.

BDD as a Result of Illness

There have been some interesting cases of BDD that have developed after some illness or trauma to the brain. Scientists call this "organic BDD." In one case, a twenty-four-year-old man showed BDD symptoms after developing an inflammation (swelling) of the brain (Gabbay et al. 2003). In another case, a twenty-one-year-old became preoccupied with the size of his ears and feet after subacute sclerosing panencephalitis (SSPC; Salib 1988). SSPC is a very rare condition in which the measles virus leads to brain damage, resulting in swelling or irritation of brain tissue. BDD has also been shown to develop after strep infections in a syndrome called PANDAS (pediatric autoimmune neuropsychiatric disorders associated with streptococcal infections; Sverd et al. 1997). It's thought that the strep infection leads to an autoimmune reaction in the body where antibodies produced by the infection can negatively impact nerve cells in the brain. Gabbay and colleagues (2003) also found that BDD developed after Bell's palsy and ulcerative colitis. We also know that a disturbance in body image can develop after damage to the right temporal lobe. These cases support the existing knowledge about the anatomy and function of our brain. Often in medicine, damage to a particular part of the brain and the resulting symptoms have allowed physicians to construct a "map" of the brain. For example, if a car accident leads to damage to one particular brain region and the person wakes up unable to remember events from the past, we can conclude that the particular brain area is somehow involved in memory. Different areas of your brain, called "pathways," perform different functions. For some functions, only one part of your brain may be involved, and, for others, several areas work in sequence or in conjunction.

Perception of Faces

Interestingly, our brain places quite a bit of importance on visual recognition and interpretation of faces. Forgetting science for a moment and just using common sense, this seems logical, right? After all, humans are social by nature, and our main form of interaction is through the face. We can recognize the face of our spouse, friend, or parent and distinguish it from a stranger's. Although we take this ability for granted, we're also able to correctly identify our own facial reflection and distinguish it from someone else. We rely partly on facial expression to help us identify the way people feel and how they react to our behavior.

People with BDD may be different from other people in how they visually perceive faces (Feusner et al. 2007). It appears that people with BDD analyze faces in piecemeal fashion rather than "holistically." This makes sense, because people with BDD tend to overfocus and scrutinize specific facial features rather than processing their face as a whole. In addition, Feusner and colleagues found that while processing faces, people with BDD also showed abnormal activity in the amygdala (which is responsible for emotions like fear and anger). Although results are preliminary, this research supports the daily experience of people with BDD when they mirror check: the overfocus on detail, the difficulty seeing a specific facial feature as related to the whole face, and the negative emotions that result. For example, a person with BDD who focuses on acne and redness in the face may be able to detect very minor changes in the size and color of a particular blemish, while family members insist they don't even see the bump or redness.

Psychological tests and tasks also seem to support this and give us more evidence regarding the biology of BDD. Studies in this area have found that people with BDD may have difficulties with certain types of tasks involving executive functioning (Hanes 1998) and memory (Deckersbach et al. 2000). *Executive functioning* refers to our ability to reason, make decisions, plan actions, think abstractly, and inhibit inappropriate impulses. Interestingly, in the Deckersbach study, people with BDD had difficulty in memory tasks because they approached the task by focusing on details rather than remembering the overall organization of the image presented. There's also evidence that people with BDD may be more likely to interpret ambiguous situations as threatening compared to people with OCD and people without any disorders (Buhlmann et al. 2002). Furthermore, people with BDD may also have difficulty identifying emotional expressions of other people (Buhlmann et al. 2004) and may inaccurately judge facial expressions as contemptuous (displaying hatred or disapproval). This inaccurate judgment of what others are feeling occurs more frequently when people with BDD visualize themselves in the scenario with another person (Buhlmann and Wilhelm 2004). How is this relevant to everyday experiences? Well, if you ever felt like people were looking at you, criticizing you, or judging you in some negative way, it may be because of these inaccurate judgments.

We want to step back from all this research for a moment and make an important point. This research does not suggest that people with BDD are "brain damaged" or not able to think or reason. All of these findings suggest that there are very subtle differences in how people with BDD process the world around them, and these subtle differences influence the development of the disorder.

Serotonin

Serotonin, one of the major chemicals (neurotransmitters) in the brain, is thought to be involved in mood, sleep, and appetite. Apparently, it also plays a role in anxiety, mood, and obsessive-compulsive spectrum disorders like BDD. Neurotransmitters are part of the communication system in the brain, allowing one nerve cell to speak to another via a chemical message. It's believed that psychiatric disorders are the result of imbalances of these chemicals in the brain. Psychiatric medications, therefore, are designed to increase or decrease specific neurotransmitters. The medications that have demonstrated improvement in BDD symptoms are serotonin reuptake inhibitors. Some common ones are fluoxetine, paroxetine, fluvoxamine, and sertraline. SRIs increase the amount of serotonin available in the brain.

Genetics

Do genetics play a role in BDD? We do have some evidence that BDD runs in families. In one study, 8 percent of people with BDD had a family member with the same diagnosis. This may not sound like a large number, but considering that approximately 2 percent of people in the general population have BDD, this is four times higher (Richter et al. 2004). Interestingly, Richter and colleagues also found that a certain gene may be linked to BDD. Unfortunately, you can't go to your doctor to be tested for the presence of BDD.

Psychological Influences

The psychological influence in the biopsychosocial model refers to our thoughts, beliefs, and perceptions about ourselves, our environment, and our experiences in life. It also refers to individual traits, such as temperament, that influence how we interact with the world around us.

Personality/Temperament

Perhaps there are personality traits, such as shyness, self-consciousness, or a tendency to avoid close social contact, that make someone more likely to develop BDD (Veale and Neziroglu 2010). *Temperament* refers to certain personality traits that are considered to be innate in an individual, meaning the person was born with certain personality features. To date, we don't know if this is the case, since a number of people would have to be followed from birth into adulthood to see if people with particular traits develop BDD.

Aesthetic Sensitivity

Some of our clients describe an inherent talent to perceive flaws in themselves and others. One theory suggests that people with BDD, possessing a more critical eye, may just have a better ability to detect very subtle differences in appearance. In fact, a few studies have found that more people with BDD had a career, training, or education in art and design (approximately 20 percent of the study participants; Lambrou 2006). Perhaps people with BDD are also born with an increased need for symmetry. Interestingly, symmetrical features are a sign of good reproductive health in many animal species. Studies have found that people with BDD may be more accurate in perceiving the size and symmetry of certain facial features than non-BDD participants (Jerome 1992; Lambrou 2006; Thomas and Goldberg 1995). We know that in order to be psychologically healthy, humans need to be a bit biased in how they view themselves and the world. They need to place more emphasis on the positive and less emphasis on the negative aspects of life. Veale and Neziroglu (2010) have suggested that perhaps people with BDD do not possess these "rose-tinted glasses" in viewing themselves. In other words, unlike people who view themselves as more attractive than they really are, people with BDD view themselves more accurately, focusing on minute details. As a consequence, people with BDD set unachievable standards of beauty and thus they become depressed, disgusted, or ashamed of the way they look. As we indicated above, more recent brain studies, using sophisticated technology to study the brain, have found that people with BDD actually focus more on details than the whole image. So the question yet to be answered is whether people with BDD possess a distortion or disturbance in perception or whether they are actually very perceptually sensitive, noticing things that people without BDD cannot. Also, it seems that people with BDD tend to view themselves as an aesthetic object; in other words, they define themselves by the way they look. The aesthetic self plays a dominant role. Think about what you think of when you think of yourself. What is the first thing that comes into your mind? Is it your career, your intellect, your kindness, your relatedness to others, your compassion, or your character? In other words, how do you define yourself (not necessarily how you would like to define yourself)?

Social Influences

The social influences in the biopsychosocial model refer to aspects from our environment that have an effect on the development and maintenance of BDD. Some of those include a history of teasing and abuse as well as how we're influenced by the people around us. Let's look at some of these aspects from our environment more closely.

History of Teasing and Abuse

Many of our clients have described teasing and bullying in childhood and particularly adolescence. Many were teased for the physical changes, including acne, occurring during puberty. Some of our male clients clearly recall being teased due to late onset of puberty. Research into the development of body image has shown a definite link between body satisfaction and teasing, as early as elementary school (Smolak 2002) and lasting into adulthood (Cash, Winstead, and Janda 1986). We all know the importance of appearance in adolescence, and it's been demonstrated that the perception of overall physical appearance appears to be the most important factor in global self-esteem, especially in industrialized nations (Levine and Smolak 2002). One study that supports this found that people with BDD recall being teased more about their appearance than about their behavior (Buhlmann et al. 2007). We do question whether someone with BDD is more likely to remember being teased due to their sensitivity, since teasing is such a common occurrence in childhood.

Abuse in childhood has also been linked to BDD. We conducted a study comparing childhood and adolescent abuse in BDD versus OCD and found that people with BDD had higher rates of emotional and sexual abuse (Neziroglu, Khemlani-Patel, and Yaryura-Tobias 2006). Didie and colleagues found similar results (2006). Perhaps other negative experiences that lead to a focus on one's body early in life can influence body image. For example, some of our clients have experienced scars caused by car accidents, acne in adolescence, or dance lessons and competitions that led them to overfocus on their bodies and weight.

Social Learning

We know that our beliefs, our values, and the way we learn are partly due to observing the world around us. Sometimes we don't even need to be directly taught; we can watch others engaging in a task and learn. If we see that someone's behavior results in a reward, then we're more likely to try out the behavior for ourselves. For example, if you notice that classmates who used a study group to prepare for a midterm exam earned "A"s, you may be more likely to use a study group for the next exam. Psychologists call this "vicarious learning."

Let's discuss perhaps the most obvious social influence on our body image—that of the media on our standard of beauty for others and ourselves. And, if television and magazines weren't bad enough, we now have the Internet to spread the message to an even greater world audience. In the wave of reality television shows, especially the various "makeover" shows, the message has become even more obvious. An unattractive woman must undergo a radical transformation in order to win her "Prince Charming." Despite our knowledge that glossy magazine photos have been altered significantly using computer graphics programs, we still feel inadequate when looking at a beautiful image of a model. We seem to believe that it's reasonable to hold ourselves to that standard! We urge you to remind yourself that all those "beautiful people" aren't the way they look in the glossy magazines. They, too, are imperfect. Start the process of body acceptance today.

Besides the individual's sociocultural environment, one's immediate environment and family can provide numerous learning opportunities as well. This type of vicarious learning gives the message that appearance is an important trait valued in society. For example, if you had an older sibling or parent who made frequent comments about the attractiveness of neighbors or celebrities, you may have received the subtle message that physical attractiveness is important. However, it seems that direct comments about body, weight, and eating are stronger sources of parental influence than just observing your parent spending a significant amount of time on improving appearance (Levine and Smolak 2002).

How BDD Develops: A Learning Theory Model

We've been working on a model integrating the biological, psychological, and social factors into a more unified theory of BDD development (Neziroglu, Khemlani-Patel, and Veale 2008; Rabinowitz, Neziroglu, and Roberts 2007). Similar theories have been developed for eating disorders, OCD, and social phobia. We've already mentioned many of the factors earlier in this chapter. We'll now present them so you can better understand their interaction and progression into BDD. This model describes how BDD may have developed from childhood/adolescent experiences and how it progressed step by step as you aged. Follow the diagram as you read about each of the factors. Try to make connections to your life and observe whether these factors influenced you. On a piece of paper or in your notebook, jot down each of the factors and, next to it, how it has affected your life. This may help you understand why you think and feel the way you do now.

How BDD Develops: A Learning Theory Model

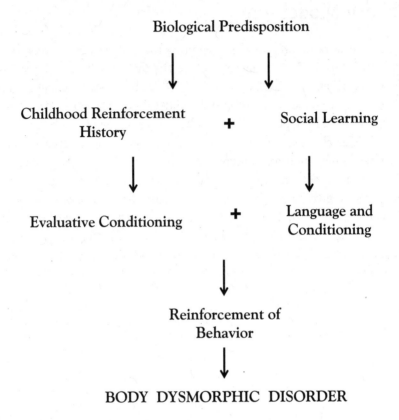

Biological Predisposition

Childhood Reinforcement History + **Social Learning**

Evaluative Conditioning + **Language and Conditioning**

Reinforcement of Behavior

BODY DYSMORPHIC DISORDER

Step 1: Biological Predisposition

As we suggested above, BDD does appear to have a biological basis. This includes brain chemistry, possible visual perception differences, genetics, and differences in brain structures. It appears that people first have to be biologically sensitive in order to develop a psychiatric condition. So, perhaps you can ask your parents and grandparents if they recall family members who suffered from some form of anxiety, depression, or OCD. Family stories will often sound something like this: "Well, your Aunt Susan was always a neat freak," or "Uncle John was a recluse and didn't attend family functions," or "There was a time when your grandmother went away for a while and we never knew why." In our consults

50

with new clients, we often gather clues about family history from accounts just like this. Speaking to a mental health professional trained in BDD can help tease out some of these other biological influences.

Step 2: Childhood Reinforcement History and Social Learning

All of the groundbreaking research being conducted suggests humans can be born with a biological vulnerability to developing certain illnesses, including BDD. But what else has influenced you, and why do life experiences trigger this biology to express itself in some people and not others? We all know that two people can grow up in the same house but develop differently. That's because we all have a unique biology and not all events affect us the same way. However, if you have the biological predisposition and a childhood history where you were rewarded or praised a lot for your appearance and maybe even got away with some mischief because you were "cute," then you may be more prone to BDD. The next step of the model suggests that early childhood history, through direct reinforcement (reward) or social learning experiences (environmental factors), gave you a subtle message regarding the importance of beauty. And this message has shaped your beliefs and values about appearance. In hundreds of conversations with our clients, we have heard countless stories about their childhood in which appearance was somehow overemphasized. For example, Larry recalls being complimented about his appearance from extended family, hearing how "handsome" and "tall" he was. Larry's family emphasized height a lot. They always commented on how tall and handsome someone was and how lucky Larry was to have taken after the tall side of the family. Tall people were, after all, more manly. (Even if this wasn't said out loud, it was implied in many subtle ways.) Larry also recalled his family comparing him to his friends in terms of his height and looks. After all, he was going to get the nice-looking girls. Even when his friend Joe, who was an excellent student but not as tall, would come over, the family would say, "Oh well, Larry may not have Joe's brains and grades, but his stunning looks will outdo any guy in the future." These messages tell children that appearance will buy them attention and praise from others and that their appearance is more important than their abilities. Obviously, most children grow up hearing how "cute" they are, especially in our current parenting culture of praise and positive reinforcement. The difference may lie in how biology and these types of life experiences combine to form our character.

Unfortunately, positive praise and reinforcement aren't the only forms of early experiences that shape our body image. As we mentioned above, negative experiences, such as physical or sexual abuse, can affect body image. Other traumas, such as car accidents that lead to scars, can result in an unnecessary amount of attention to physical appearance.

Another part of understanding how you might have developed BDD is to see how much you were affected by observing and hearing people's comments about the appearance of others. Observing how others are positively reinforced for appearance (attractive celebrities becoming rich and famous) can have a strong impact. Children and adolescents are taught that physical attractiveness is necessary for success and are bombarded with advertisements for products and cosmetic procedures to help achieve this goal. Perhaps your social learning came from observing your immediate family surroundings. If you had a parent who repeatedly pointed out TV stars' teeth or your friend's straight shiny hair or if you had a teacher who paid more attention to the good-looking kids, these experiences may also have shaped your view of appearance.

Step 3: Evaluative Conditioning

Now that you have identified possible early life experiences that laid the foundation for your values and beliefs about appearance, the next step in the model may explain how these factors came together to form BDD symptoms. If you're familiar with the famous psychology experiments of Pavlov and his dogs, then you may recall that he trained dogs to salivate at the sound of a bell. Dogs just naturally salivate when presented with food, but Pavlov rang a bell whenever food was served to these dogs so that food and bell became paired. Soon the dogs learned that the bell signaled food, and they would salivate even if food wasn't presented. Prior to this experiment, the dogs wouldn't have paid any special attention to the bell; in essence, it would have been a meaningless neutral stimulus, a nonevent, in their life. But after numerous pairings of bell and food, their brains formed a connection between the bell and food. As a result, the bell alone was able to elicit a response similar to their response to food. *Classical conditioning or learning* usually refers to reflexive or automatic physical responses not under conscious control, such as salivating or eye blinking.

There is another form of conditioning similar to this called *evaluative conditioning*, which refers to the connection formed between previously neutral stimuli and an emotional evaluation. This concept will become clear as we give you examples to illustrate. Certain life experiences, such as being teased, having acne, or reaching puberty early, can result in anxiety, depression, disgust, or shame. These life events are like the dog food in Pavlov's experiments leading to salivation. These events automatically lead not to a reflexive response, but to an emotional response. Now imagine that the teasing or abuse becomes associated with a body part. Suddenly there's a connection between these two experiences, both of which lead to shame, depression, anxiety, and other negative emotions. Here's another example of evaluative conditioning: imagine that you're being teased about your big head and you feel ashamed, and thereafter you dislike or feel ashamed of anything, such as your hairline, that you associate with your head. Because the teasing is evaluated as unpleasant, all paired associations are also deemed unpleasant. In other words, you associate your hairline with the teasing about your head, and both then take on a negative evaluation and elicit the same response of shame.

LANGUAGE AND CONDITIONING

Although evaluative conditioning and early life experiences shape all our individual thoughts, behaviors, and emotions, we have one other skill—language—that helps develop our beliefs about appearance. That's right, *language*, our ability to talk and formulate thoughts. How language helps us develop beliefs is explained by relational frame theory (RFT). RFT, developed by Steven Hayes and his colleagues (2001), is a complex theory that would require an entire three-hundred-page book to explain and has already been done quite well by Dr. Hayes! We'll attempt to briefly review a few of the major ideas and how we can apply the theory to BDD.

RFT states that our language ability allows us to represent events, ideas, objects, and memories in our mind simply with words. These words can trigger emotions. Try this simple exercise: imagine warm, gooey, freshly baked chocolate chip cookies. What thoughts, images, and memories did this image trigger? Maybe you recalled a parent baking desserts, a cooking class in school, or a grandmother cooking Sunday dinner. If we asked what emotions this simple image brought, you may have experienced happiness, a feeling of nostalgia, contentment, hunger, or even regret or sadness. Even if you've never baked cookies, your ability to represent ideas mentally through language allowed you to make an association between cookies and other events. You didn't even need to be in a kitchen at this exact moment to experience the event. Only humans have this ability.

Now let's apply this to BDD. Language helps form connections in our mind between events through complex networks of associated ideas, images, and evaluations. Phrases like "similar to," "bigger than," and "before and after" allow us to connect and compare things mentally without actual experience. For example, a child could learn that having a pimple is associated with disgust, and so later in life any blemish elicits disgust. The word "pimple" is similar to blemish, acne, bumps on face, or unsmooth face and thus those similar words alone can elicit the same negative emotions. This is why people with BDD may respond in a negative manner to any event or word that reminds them of a similar situation. For example, if they have a disgust reaction at one point to a pimple, thoughts of anything similar to it may elicit the same reaction. If they had been teased about their big head, then the word "big" could evoke an unpleasant feeling. Likewise, any similar associated body part (hairline/hair) could elicit the same response.

Perhaps in the case of BDD, humans make arbitrary associations between appearance, social success, and/or undesirable human traits. For example, your mother has complained about your cousin who's a troublemaker in school and how your aunt is having such difficulties with him. Your mother may say to you, "What a pity your cousin is such a nuisance and a poor student, when he is such a good-looking boy and he has so many friends." Have you ever been stunned by some of the comments people make—comments like "Wow, she had such a horrible life and she's so pretty"? What do you think we learn from and associate with these comments? We learn that somehow people who are good-looking should succeed in school, have a wonderful career, and lead an exemplary life. No wonder as young adults we compare ourselves to these people. Hopefully, at some point we begin to realize that there's no relationship between looks and grades, or looks and good behavior, or looks and acceptance by friends.

These interpretations of life experiences may foster BDD beliefs, such as *If I'm attractive, I will be more likely to obtain what I want, Being attractive is the most important thing in the world, I need to be noticed, Life is not worth living unless I am attractive,* and so on. It's also during this time that attention is drawn to the perceived flawed body part. Selective attention to the flaw leads to more focus on it and thus a strengthening of the conditioning process.

See if you can remember any words that make you think of positive or negative attributes of yourself, such as big = ugly; tall = athletic, manly; acne = rejection by others.

Step 4: How Behavior Is Reinforced

The last step in the model explains how BDD beliefs and behaviors are maintained and strengthened. As BDD develops through adolescence and into adulthood, people typically engage in certain behaviors. As you read in chapter 1, these involve such behaviors as mirror checking, camouflaging, using cosmetic products, and seeking reassurance. But how do these behaviors continue and worsen? They're maintained via *operant conditioning principles*. Okay, these fancy words basically mean that we reduce our uncomfortable feelings by doing certain things, such as spending hours straightening our hair to get it just right.

Operant conditioning is linked with a famous psychologist by the name of B. F. Skinner. Skinner believed that human beings (and animals) learn a behavior through a system of rewards and punishments that are part of the person's immediate environment. Skinner proposed, and later demonstrated, that when a researcher manipulates the rewards and punishments in the environment, subjects can learn (and unlearn) behavior. In behavioral terms, a *reinforcement* (reward) refers to anything that causes a behavior to increase, while a *punishment* is something that causes a behavior to decrease. If a person's environment rewards a behavior, this increases the likelihood that the person will repeat the same behavior in the future. Conversely, if the person's environment punishes a particular behavior, this decreases the likelihood the behavior will be repeated. To illustrate, imagine that you smile at a classmate every day in the hallway. Your classmate smiles back, which leads to pleasant feelings that serve as positive reinforcement. Therefore, it's more likely that you'll smile at this classmate and others in the future.

Positive experiences increase the likelihood of certain behaviors, but so does the removal of negative experiences. This form of reinforcement is called *negative reinforcement*. For example, engaging in mirror checking, camouflaging, and, most clearly, avoidance of public situations results in a feeling of security and relief for a person with BDD. These behaviors take away negative emotions and, therefore, are likely to continue. People with BDD may engage in a variety of behaviors as they attempt to reduce disgust, anxiety, or negative feelings in general.

Can you think of anything you've done over and over again that has taken away your negative feelings? Some examples may be mirror checking, using a lot of foundation, spending excessive time on your hair to get it right, or shaving every part of your body. These are only a few examples of behaviors that usually help reduce negative emotions and are thus known to be negatively reinforcing.

In conclusion, a number of complex factors influence the development of BDD. We hope this chapter has helped you identify your own personal influences and understand BDD better.

3

Why Should You
Seek Treatment?

Making the decision to seek psychological and/or psychiatric treatment can be an intimidating one. There are a number of potential obstacles, including the pragmatic ones, such as tracking down a professional familiar with BDD, finding the time for weekly sessions, and having the financial resources to pay for therapy. Sometimes those obstacles can be more easily resolved than the fears and apprehension about the treatment process itself. If you've never seen a therapist before, perhaps you're concerned about being able to find a professional you can comfortably share your intimate thoughts and experiences with. If you've had difficulty being understood by others, you may naturally feel hesitant to share your story with one more person. You may also be confused how psychological treatment is going to fix a problem of physical appearance. In this chapter, we'll discuss ways to overcome some of these obstacles and review the reasons why and how treatment may be beneficial to you. The first step in helping yourself is to see how BDD has affected your life.

EXERCISE: How Has BDD Impacted Your Life?

Can you think back to a time in your life when you were not as concerned with your appearance? What was daily life like then, and how has it changed since then? We urge you to take a look at the list below and reflect on how your struggle with appearance has impacted your life. The list includes some of the most common changes people report. Check off the ones that apply to you. If you've experienced other changes that are not on this list, please add them to the list.

_____ I have less friends now.

_____ My friends no longer call me.

_____ I go out less frequently.

_____ I feel uncomfortable when I do go out.

_____ I spend most of my time worried about my appearance rather than being with family and friends.

_____ I take risks that I ordinarily would not take (for example, checking reflection in rearview mirror while driving, using cosmetic products that can damage my skin).

_____ I no longer can engage in sports.

Now in your notebook under the title "How My Life Has Changed," write down some other things that have changed in your life.

Now that you have reflected on how your life has changed, take some time to think about what you wish your life could be like. Try the following exercise to create your wish list.

EXERCISE: My Wish List for My Life

Make a list of things you'd like to have in your life. Here are some common wishes:

- I wish I could date.

- I wish I could go back to school.

- I wish I could work.

- I wish I could enjoy life.

- I wish I could "think" less.

- I wish I could move out.

- I wish I could post my photo online and increase my social networking.

- I wish I could spend less on cosmetic and medical products.

- I wish I could be more social.

We hope this exercise helps you reflect on the changes in your quality of life as a result of BDD. You may have experienced anxiety imagining yourself engaging in some of the above tasks, despite a desire to move forward in your life. Many people with BDD feel the same way and hold off on important life changes or events due to their anxiety. Perhaps the single clearest reason to seek treatment is to improve your quality of life. Live the life you want, not the one BDD dictates.

Research has shown that people with BDD unfortunately have a very poor quality of life, which can be lower than people suffering from depression or medical conditions, such as diabetes. This may sound quite discouraging, but the reality is that you can receive proper treatment and change your life, as many others with BDD have done.

Jen was a thirty-three-year-old client with BDD who focused on her hair texture and the overall shape of her face. At the time she entered therapy, she lived with her parents and worked two days a week. She was quite ashamed of and frustrated with her dependence on her parents and her lack of a romantic relationship. Her distress about her life circumstances was as difficult for her as her BDD symptoms. In the first few months of treatment, however, she learned to accept her current life circumstances and focus first on improving her daily BDD compulsions and thoughts. She stayed committed to decreasing her symptoms and was gradually able to socialize more, improve her confidence and functioning at work, and become more independent. After a year of therapy and medications, Jen slowly began achieving her long-term goals. She was able to exercise at a gym without anxiety, she moved out of her parents' home, increased her work schedule, and even added in a weekly volunteer job. Now she plans to complete her master's degree in education, which she had given up when her symptoms worsened.

Although a year may sound like a very long time to wait for life to improve, many of the positive steps in treatment are cumulative and help an individual maintain hope and motivation throughout the process.

The Role of Cosmetic Surgery and Dermatology Procedures

According to the American Society for Aesthetic Plastic Surgery, over 10.2 million cosmetic surgical and nonsurgical procedures were performed in the United States in 2008. This is a 162 percent increase since the society began collecting data in 1997. In terms of the cost, the general population of the United States spent just under $12 billion on cosmetic procedures: $7.2 billion for surgical and $4.6 billion for nonsurgical procedures.

So, what does this suggest? First, it suggests that the search for beauty in the United States is quite common, and, second, it's certainly a large financial industry! So you say to yourself, *Why not me? I know plenty of people who go for surgery or want to go. Others seem pleased with the results, so why shouldn't I try to improve my appearance?* You are absolutely right that many people who go for cosmetic surgery feel better afterward about their appearance. But here is the bad news. The research shows that those who have BDD aren't satisfied after surgery and in fact many often feel worse. There's a big difference between the way people with BDD and people without BDD feel after cosmetic surgery. Although some people with BDD have viewed their body part slightly more favorably after surgery, they didn't experience a change in their daily distress over their appearance. In essence, although you may feel somewhat satisfied with the outcome of surgery, your BDD symptoms won't change. Perhaps you'll become focused on another body part or feel you want to pursue a second surgery because the results didn't meet your expectations. If you've invested a lot of time, energy, and money to have the surgery or procedure and still don't feel satisfied, there's a risk you'll feel more hopeless than before the surgery. What we usually advise is that you give yourself at least a few months of proper cognitive behavioral therapy before you make the decision.

If you've been consulting with dermatologists and surgeons, you may have realized the pitfalls that can occur as a result of these visits. Have you felt discouraged or frustrated after the visit? Has the appointment left you feeling even more unattractive? Many clients we've treated feel the same way. In our practice, we've often accompanied our clients to these appointments to learn more about the process and to help our clients. We've observed the following: (1) Cosmetic surgeons and dermatologists are trained to find the smallest imperfections—imperfections that the average person doesn't notice. You may leave the appointment believing that since the surgeon can see the imperfections, then everyone else can too. This may make you feel even more self-conscious and distressed. (2) Since surgeons do focus on details, they may even suggest other procedures or point out imperfections that you didn't previously notice. Again, you may leave more upset about your appearance. (3) Since cosmetic surgeons will likely want to make you feel understood and provide you with excellent customer service, they may agree to do a procedure even if it's unnecessary. A surgeon's agreement to perform the surgery may lead you to believe that the surgeon also thinks your body part is unattractive. (4) Dermatologists may make recommendations to alter your lifestyle to improve your appearance. These may include using specific skin products, avoiding certain foods, using only clean towels or even certain color towels on your face, washing your hands frequently, and so on. Unfortunately, these suggestions can be mistaken for absolute rules and can cause you to spend an unnecessary amount of time and money following them. For all of these reasons, we caution individuals with BDD to limit their visits to cosmetic surgeons and dermatologists. If you can, find a dermatologist who is knowledgeable about BDD and therefore able to be sensitive and empathetic to your needs.

Based on our clinical experience and our knowledge of BDD, we can confidently advise you to avoid surgery for your appearance. If you do choose to go through with it, we suggest that you do so cautiously. We also offer you the following suggestions: (1) Use the support of a therapist to help you deal with any negative thoughts and feelings you may experience before and after the procedure. (2) Ask a trusted friend or family member to accompany you to all appointments. (3) Find a physician familiar with BDD. (4) Don't agree to procedures that will drastically change your appearance.

The Role of Family When Seeking Treatment

If you're currently ambivalent about seeking treatment, we can safely guess that a loved one, either friend or family member, at some point has suggested you pursue psychological or psychiatric treatment. Perhaps a loved one has even gone far enough to initiate an appointment and accompanied you to sessions. If you've felt forced into treatment, we understand your reluctance in continuing. If you're not ready to discuss your appearance-related concerns, then we urge you to make this clearly known to your therapist or psychiatrist. There may be other issues you feel comfortable discussing, such as your unhappiness with your current social life, your anxiety, or depression. Find a therapist who's willing to offer therapy at your pace. Spend some time in the first couple of sessions expressing your reluctance to talk about your appearance and perhaps develop some goals for therapy that you're ready at the present moment to work on. Perhaps you want help finding a part-time job, or you would like to eat at restaurants more often than you do. Ask a therapist's help in achieving these initial goals. If you're having difficulties with your family, then setting up some joint sessions with your family may resolve the conflict. If your family members are confused about your anxiety and depression about your appearance, a therapist may be able to explain how difficult your life is. In short, a therapist can be an effective advocate for you.

We hope that you have found your own reasons to seek treatment after reading this chapter. In the next chapter, we'll prepare you for the treatment process.

4

What Should You Expect in Treatment?

Now that you've looked at reasons why someone may seek treatment, you may seriously be considering entering therapy. But where do you go? How do you find someone who's right for you? How do you prepare?

Finding a Therapist

We think that the strategies we present in this book can be very useful in helping you with your BDD. Finding a therapist who fits the bill is important, too. Here's a list of some organizations in English-speaking countries that can be helpful resources for finding a therapist who knows how to treat BDD:

- Anxiety Disorders Association of America (adaa.org)

- Anxiety Disorders Association of Canada (anxietycanada.ca)

- Anxiety Disorders Association of Victoria, Inc. (www.adavic.org .au)

- Anxiety Treatment Australia (www.anxietyaustralia.com.au)

- Australian Association for Cognitive and Behaviour Therapy (aacbt.org)

- Association for Behavioral and Cognitive Therapies (abct.org)

- Association for Contextual Behavioral Science (contextual psychology.org)

- BDD Foundation (thebddfoundation.com)

- BDD Central (www.bddcentral.com)

- British Association for Behavioural and Cognitive Psycho-therapies (www.babcp.com)

- International OCD Foundation (www.ocfoundation.org)

- OCD Action (www.ocdaction.org.uk)

- OCD Ireland (ocdireland.org)

If you don't find a therapist in your area on one of these websites, don't be discouraged. We suggest that you see if any local hospitals have treatment facilities for OCD. Since BDD is an obsessive-compulsive spectrum disorder, you may find someone who treats BDD at one of those facilities. If you're unable to find a provider locally, you still have other options. Nowadays many therapists offer alternate methods of communication, such as using the Internet or phone sessions. In addition, you may need to go out of your area for a few weeks for intensive treatment. Some places are inpatient, requiring you to stay in a hospital, while others are outpatient and you stay in accommodations outside of the treatment facility.

To help you find a therapist who will be a good fit for you, ask potential therapists these questions:

- What type of therapy do you do?

- What techniques do you use to treat BDD? (Do not ask if they do a particular type of therapy. Let them tell you what they do. You want to hear that they have training and experience using cognitive behavioral therapy (CBT). Other buzzwords and phrases are "exposure and response prevention" and "cognitive therapy." If they just stop at these key phrases, ask them to give examples of these treatments. You want to hear them say something about challenging irrational or anxious thoughts, doing exercises or experiments to test your thoughts, and trying different things that you've been avoiding.)

- What is your training and experience in treating BDD? How many people with BDD have you seen?

- Are you willing to leave the office during sessions? Do you do home visits? (Effective exposure and response prevention may require leaving the office or even doing some sessions in your home or elsewhere.)

- Do you have extended office hours? Do you have night appointments? (Consider asking this question if it's tough for you to get out during the daytime due to your symptoms.)

- If I'm having a tough time getting to the office, can you do phone sessions or videochat? (Although phone sessions or videochat aren't a healthy or good option for your whole course of treatment, having a therapist who's flexible and understanding enough to allow some phone or videochat sessions indicates that the therapist is well versed in the difficulties you may experience. At the beginning of treatment, when it may be very difficult to get out or face people, using the phone or videochat is a good option. Many times we've sat with our clients in their cars to do a few sessions, or we've gone to their homes. Flexibility is key.)

Treatment Frequency

How often would you have to attend therapy? Most often people think of therapy sessions as being forty-five to fifty minutes once a week. Sessions can actually be several hours per day, multiple days per week; they also can be part of an outpatient, residential, or hospital-based program. How often you attend treatment really depends on a few different factors: How severe is your BDD? Do you have another diagnosis (such as depression)? Are you suicidal? How quickly do you need to get better? In our experience, most people with BDD initially need a few sessions a week to get going. However, as they improve, the frequency decreases; eventually they meet for hour-long sessions once a week.

Getting Motivated

We're going to be up-front with you. Therapy can be tough. Treatment for BDD is action oriented. That means that you can expect to do more than just talk about how your week went and how you felt about it. But it's definitely worth it. Therapy is like going to a personal trainer. If you wanted to get fit and employed a personal trainer to help you out for an hour a week, would you expect to see results if you only exercised when you were with your trainer? Of course not! When you work your body, it's expected that you'll also exercise regularly and engage in some related behaviors, such as eating a healthy, balanced diet. When you work your mind, you have to put in the same effort to get results.

We want to ensure that you're ready and motivated for the journey that you're about to take. Since you're reading this book, you probably already have some level of motivation to work on your BDD. But you may also have some remaining concerns about how effective treatment will be, if you'll be able to follow through with it, or if you can change. Rest assured, any concerns that you may have have been expressed by others before you. We want to help you explore and challenge these concerns in order to increase your motivation. The next exercise will do just that.

EXERCISE: List the Pros and Cons

Okay, let's get started with the pros and cons of changing: how will you benefit from change, and what obstacles will you face? We're sure you've done this with other areas of your life where you had to make a decision. Get out your notebook and make two columns and label one "Pros" and the other "Cons." Spend some time thinking of as many things as you can. Here are some examples from our clients who've done this exercise:

Pros	Cons
I won't worry as much about my looks.	I'll feel anxious doing therapy.
I'll be able to go out without spending so much time on my appearance.	I'll let myself go because I won't be paying as much attention to the way that I look.

Sometimes it's hard to figure out the whole list in one sitting. We suggest that you make this an ongoing list, adding new pros or cons as you think of them.

Strategies for Change

Waiting for change, especially when you're trying so hard, can be tough. We've outlined some strategies to motivate you and help you stay motivated for change.

Educate Yourself

Learn about BDD and your particular symptoms. Be aware of your thoughts, behaviors, and feelings. The more aware you are, the more motivated you'll be to change because you'll realize how BDD has held you back from pursuing the life you want.

Be Patient

We know that waiting for change can be difficult. People often expect change to come instantaneously, especially when it comes to how they feel. But it's important to remember that change takes time, whether it be with your BDD symptoms or with something else.

Have you ever vacationed in a foreign country, watched a movie with subtitles, or just heard some people speaking another language on the street and thought, *I would love to know how to speak another language?* Unfortunately, a week in France won't make you fluent. You might be able to get by with learning *bonjour, merci, au revoir,* and some other simple phrases. However, if you really want to learn a language, you have to be dedicated to it. You have to set goals, study, do homework, read books, listen to instructional CDs or MP3s, and maybe even take classes or private lessons. No matter what, you have to put some work into it. Wanting to learn a language isn't enough to actually learn it. The same applies to treatment. Whether you decide to use this book as a guide or you choose to enter treatment, or even if you do both, you'll need to do the work—and it'll take some time to see results.

Reward Yourself

So we've established that making changes takes time and dedication. While working on your BDD symptoms is crucial, giving yourself a pat on the back is just as important. Lots of times people with BDD have dropped out of life, and the fun and pleasurable things usually to go down the tubes as well. So, just as it's important to schedule time to work on your BDD exercises, it's also important to reward yourself. Now the thing is, you want to reward yourself *after* you work on some techniques. Think about it. If you give yourself the reward before you do a chore, you probably won't get to that chore. We suggest that you give yourself some incentives for making steps toward overcoming your BDD. This next exercise will help you identify those incentives.

EXERCISE: How Can You Reward Yourself?

You've already started to pave the way for your treatment by reading this book and doing the exercises. Good for you! As you continue going through this book, plan ahead and schedule time for the exercises. We suggest that you schedule time every day. We'll talk about how much time you need for these exercises when we address treatment later on in the book. But for now, take out your notebook and brainstorm some rewards and fun activities that you can use to motivate you.

Do you find that you aren't doing the fun things you used to do? Have you stopped spending time with friends, stopped going to the gym, to the movies, out to eat? Make a list of the things that you love to do that have fallen by the wayside.

At first, what used to be a reward may feel like a chore (for example, you may love going to the movies, but your BDD symptoms get in the way). If this is the case, choose some simpler rewards for now—just some things that you can easily do around the house. Part of treatment is to start doing the things that you love or that you think you'll love. Here are some ideas to get you started:

- Eat your favorite food.

- Listen to music.

- Watch your favorite movie or television show.

- Take a bath.

- Allow yourself to download a special song.

- Get into a chat room.

- Play a computer game.

Now that you've listed a few rewards, choose one and do it. You've put time in reading the first few chapters. Now practice rewarding yourself!

Set Realistic Goals

A common trap for people with BDD (and lots of people in general) is setting unrealistic goals. For instance, entirely changing the way you look is unrealistic. So is expecting that you'll be 100 percent better by reading this book in an afternoon. Establishing practical and attainable goals is needed in order to be successful with anything in life, especially reducing BDD symptoms. The next exercise will help you with your goal setting.

EXERCISE: What Are Your Goals?

We've emphasized the importance of goal setting. It's time to get out that notebook and write down your goals for treatment. We also find it helpful when people set short- and long-term goals, so write down your goals for the next three months, six months, one year, and five years. Some early goals of treatment will be to help you achieve a sense of accomplishment and feel hopeful that treatment works. So keep your goals realistic and reasonable. Here are some examples of goals:

Goals for the Next Three Months

- Get out of the house once a day.

- Go out to eat with my family where people I know are unlikely to be.

- Reduce the time I spend in front of the mirror checking my appearance.

Goals for the Next Six Months

- Go out one or two full days a week without camouflaging myself.

- Maintain new behaviors that have been established in treatment.

Goals for the Next Year

- Go back to school.

- Be open to a romantic relationship.

Goals for the Next Five Years

- Get married.

- Buy a house.

Not only is it important to settle on goals, but it's also important to anticipate what obstacles may get in the way. The more aware you are of these hurdles, the better you can deal with them. The next exercise will help you identify some of the obstacles you may face.

EXERCISE: Treatment Obstacles

What may be some obstacles to your treatment? Below we've listed some obstacles to treatment that we see all the time. Look them over, and then list the obstacles that you anticipate you'll encounter in treatment.

- Not doing homework

- Not having enough time

- Canceling therapy sessions

- Constantly arguing with the therapist

- Getting discouraged

- Not believing that therapy can change body image

- Wanting results immediately

While some of these potential pitfalls are specific to treatment with a therapist, it's also worthwhile to examine how they can affect you as you go through this self-help book. Being aware of these obstacles can help you address them before they become problems. Let's move on to some topics that will come up in therapy—assessment and medication.

Assessment

When you start therapy, your clinician may ask you to fill out several questionnaires to get a better sense of what will help in therapy, where to start, and so on. During this process, you may learn that, in addition to BDD, you have other problems that need to be addressed. For instance, if you have severe depression, are suicidal, or have a substance use problem, you'll need to tackle that first. The assessment process helps prioritize your treatment goals and the order in which you accomplish them.

Medication

In addition to cognitive behavioral therapy, medications are often used to make it easier for people with BDD to cope with anxiety and depression. Many people find they also make it easier to go through the treatment process. Although it's not a must to be on medication, it's often helpful. Of course, it's important that you be given the right prescription with the right dosage and for the right length of time. So if you've tried medications and they haven't helped you in the past, it could be for many reasons. It's always worth trying to find the right one for you.

Serotonin-reuptake inhibitors (SRIs or SSRIs) are antidepressant medications that also work on decreasing obsessions and compulsions, which are a large part of BDD. People are often confused by these medications because they're referred to as antidepressants. You may say, "Yeah, I feel depressed sometimes, but the real problem is that I'm anxious and thinking about my BDD 24/7! What's an antidepressant going to do for that?" In addition to depression, SRIs are used for a wide variety of disorders, including social phobias, panic disorder, posttraumatic stress disorder, and some eating disorders. They also help decrease anxiety.

Dosages of medications for BDD tend to be high. That's why it's extremely important to disclose your BDD symptoms so that you and your physician can monitor them appropriately. The amount of an SRI needed to treat depression tends to be lower than for BDD. So if you are only focusing on your depression, you may not be getting the dosage you need to really help your BDD.

Be patient when you begin to take a new medication. SRIs don't act instantaneously. They may take up to twelve to sixteen weeks to start being effective. We know that this is quite a long time and that the wait can be very frustrating. It's extremely important that you stick with it.

Have you tried a particular medication and given it up because of side effects or because it didn't seem to be working? Don't be discouraged. You just need to find the right medication for you. Make sure you have the proper dosage, and stay on the medication even if it seems as if it's not working. Here is a list of the SRIs available in the United States:

- Fluoxetine (Prozac)

- Sertraline (Zoloft)

- Citalopram (Celexa)

- Escitalopram (Lexapro)

- Paroxetine (Paxil)

- Fluvoxamine (Luvox)

- Clomipramine (Anafranil)

What if you try an SRI and it does not work? Well, first, as we explained, you want to be on an adequate dose for an adequate time. Remember, it can take a while for these medications to work. The next step would be to try another SRI. Where one may not work for you, another may. Another strategy may be to add another medication, such as another SRI, an antipsychotic, or a benzodiazepine. These options should be discussed further with your prescribing physician.

Many factors can play into the decision of whether to try therapy or medication or both. We feel that therapy and medication complement each other. For instance, medication can make it easier to engage in treatment if you feel too anxious, depressed, or suicidal to be motivated for therapy. While we feel that taking medication depends on many factors and is a personal decision, we do feel strongly that someone with severe symptoms of BDD, depression, or suicidal thoughts should be on medication.

Understandably, considering taking medication may be scary. People worry about how medications affect them. Some hesitate because they feel that medication is unnatural or that it can damage the brain. There has been no evidence to show that SRIs will hurt your brain. Serotonin is a chemical that occurs naturally in your brain, and SRIs are prescribed to correct the "chemical imbalance," not create any damage. In fact, SRIs have been shown to prevent brain cells from dying and can help in the growth of new brain cells (Jacobs, Van Praag, and Gage 2000).

Now you know how to look for a therapist and have a sense of what to expect in the initial steps of therapy. Let's look next at the nitty-gritty of your BDD treatment strategies and techniques, which are addressed in the following treatment chapters.

5

Cognitive Therapy

Changing Troubling Beliefs about Your Body

Y ou've been patiently reading the last four chapters to learn all about BDD. But your main reason for purchasing this book is probably to learn how you can feel better. As we've mentioned before, effective treatments are available for BDD. They typically involve a mix of strategies, many of which we'll introduce in the next few chapters. A combination of professional guidance and self-help is usually the best approach. We do understand that it's not always easy to seek professional help. If possible, you may find it helpful to work with a therapist in addition to using this book, especially if your BDD is severe.

How does one tackle all of the suffering that comes with the diagnosis? Since you now have a thorough understanding of BDD and have made lists of your own symptoms and life experiences, the next step is to begin the process of tackling these symptoms and changing certain patterns in your daily life. *Behavior therapy strategies* aim to change behaviors or actions, while *cognitive therapy* aims to change the beliefs that contribute to your distress. In the end, though, both work together to reduce your negative feelings so that you can practice living a more balanced life. Almost all cognitive behavioral therapists with expertise in treating BDD will start with cognitive therapy. In our experience, this approach makes our clients feel the most comfortable, so that's where we'll begin.

Cognitive therapy's philosophy is not really new. As you read on, you may realize that you've heard aspects of cognitive therapy all around you. We've all heard such inspirational statements as "Change your attitude to change your life," "Visualize success and you will achieve it," and so on. Sayings like this are common on television, in inspirational novels and biographies, and in self-help books for weight loss, career success, and finding the perfect mate. So, you may be asking yourself, *Then why should I bother reading this chapter? I've tried thinking positive already, and it hasn't cured my BDD.*

So why should you read this chapter? Because cognitive therapy is a systematic and consistent approach to changing your thoughts and beliefs. The goal is to view things in a more rational and realistic way. The goal is *not* to be happy! That's right; you read the previous sentence correctly. Good cognitive therapy doesn't necessarily attempt to make you happy in five easy steps; instead it teaches you how to approach both negative and positive life experiences in a more balanced way. Hopefully, the more that you practice realistic balanced thinking, the more in control you'll be of your negative emotions and thoughts. Ultimately, this will lead to a sense of inner peace. You'll struggle less with worries and negative perceptions of yourself, others, the world, and your future.

Research about cognitive therapy for BDD suggests it's a highly effective approach. Cognitive therapy alone, behavioral therapy alone, or a combination of the two has been shown to improve BDD symptoms significantly (Butters and Cash 1987; Campisi 1995; Geremia and Neziroglu 2001; Khemlani-Patel, Neziroglu, and Mancusi 2011; Neziroglu et al. 1996; O'Grady 2002; Veale et al. 1996). In fact, psychological therapy may be more effective than medication (Williams, Hadjistavropoulos, and Sharpe 2006). So, let's get started learning the steps of cognitive therapy.

Step 1: Identify Your Internal Dialogue

Cognitive therapy techniques are best learned by using a pen and notebook, so keep both handy as you read this chapter and try the strategies. The first step in cognitive therapy is to identify and be aware of your internal dialogue. We all have thoughts, perceptions, opinions, and so on running through our minds all day. Many individuals, however, spend much of the day unaware of these thoughts, and they underestimate the degree to which these thoughts can truly influence daily life.

How you perceive events in your day, even minuscule ones, can impact your mood and behavior. The next time you're in a long line at the grocery store, take special note of the people around you. Perhaps one person sighs impatiently, looking at her watch, and rudely asking the cashier to hurry up, while another person in line calmly browses *People* magazine! Why is it that every person reacts differently to exactly the same situation? Cognitive therapy suggests that our inner perceptions, beliefs, and thoughts are to blame. If we can pretend to read minds for a moment, we can make an educated guess that the impatient customer in line was having very different thoughts than the customer reading a magazine. Perhaps the first is saying to herself, *I can't believe this cashier is so incompetent! I'll be late to work and have a horrible day*, while the person reading a magazine may be thinking, *This is annoying, but I expect this to happen once in a while, so I might as well read a magazine to pass the time.*

Cognitive therapy will *not* teach you to react to negative events with positive thoughts. So, if you were standing in that long line, we wouldn't expect you to say, "Great! I'm thrilled to be standing in a long line and be late to work!" It *will* teach you to replace extreme negative thoughts and conclusions with more rational ones. So, if the first customer was our client in treatment, we might challenge her prediction that she will definitely have a horrible day since that would be a hypothetical prediction rather than absolute fact. We would coach her to recognize that negative experiences can be put on a continuum from wonderful to awful. Being late may be inconvenient, but it's not the biggest tragedy in one's life. Also, by thinking more rationally, she would be more likely to come up with solutions to the situation—for example, to call a colleague and say she'll be late or to ask someone to cover for her for five or ten minutes.

Although this is a trivial example, it's important to note that these kinds of trivial incidents and our negative perceptions of them can have a cumulative impact on our daily mood. Learning to take a step back and reminding yourself to challenge your black-or-white, all-or-nothing thinking, your tendency to make predictions without sufficient evidence, and your jumping to conclusions about what others are thinking can have a significant impact on your life.

At this point, like many of the people we've treated, you may question how changing your thoughts can be of any value to you when your suffering is due to a "physical problem." Remember what we said in chapter 1: we all have a mental representation of the way we look. What cognitive therapy does is help you change the mental image you have. We recognize that you might be skeptical. But learning cognitive therapy strategies can improve life for anyone, regardless of gender, life experiences, or struggles. All humans, to some extent, suffer from moments of extreme negative thinking. The strategies in this chapter can guide you in improving your daily mood and hopefully decreasing your suffering. A good way to start is by completing the exercise below.

EXERCISE: Identifying Automatic Thoughts

This exercise will help you identify your inner dialogue as well as help reveal the extent to which your thoughts may affect how you feel about your looks. There are two parts to this exercise: in the first, you'll do some people watching, and in the second, you'll look at a magazine.

People Watching

Set aside half a day when the mall or some other public place is crowded. (A beach, the town pool, or a lake where people swim would be particularly great for this exercise.) Take a field trip to your chosen location and bring a notepad and pen. Find a comfortable place where you can observe others and reflect without being disturbed. Follow these steps:

1. Look around at the crowd. Take special notice of people who typically make you feel insecure, anxious, sad, or self-conscious.

2. Write down any negative thoughts and beliefs that pop into your head.

3. Are you comparing yourself to these people? Are you coming to any conclusions about their life based on their looks? Are you judging them based on their overall appearance or any special aspects of their appearance?

4. Congratulate yourself for doing something that may bring up some uncomfortable feelings! This list of thoughts will be important and useful as we progress through cognitive therapy.

5. Put the list away and take it out in a day or two. Do you notice any patterns to your thoughts? Are many of these statements and beliefs similar to each other? If so, how? Write down your observations.

6. Save this list to use in a future exercise.

Magazine Watching

Find a magazine with glossy photos of attractive people, such as a fashion, fitness, or health magazine. Then follow these steps:

1. Choose four photos of people who, in your opinion, are very attractive. Choose two of your gender and two of the opposite gender.

2. Using sticky notes, jot down any thoughts that pop into your mind as you look at each photo. Place the sticky notes by the corresponding photos.

3. Are you comparing yourself to the people in the photos? Are you coming to any conclusions about their life based on their appearance? Are you judging them based on their overall appearance or any special aspects of their appearance?

4. Congratulate yourself for doing something that may bring up some uncomfortable feelings! This list of thoughts will be important and useful as we progress through cognitive therapy.

5. Put the list away and take it out in a day or two. Do you notice any patterns to your thoughts? Are many of these statements and beliefs similar to each other? If so, how? Write down any of these observations as well.

6. Save this list to use in a future exercise.

In order to continue the process of cognitive change, keep a regular diary of your thoughts. The two parts of the exercise above were designed to deliberately place you in uncomfortable situations in order to elicit negative thoughts, but keeping a daily record of thoughts allows you to identify and ultimately challenge and replace negative thoughts with more balanced ones. The thought record form below is typically used by cognitive therapists. Fill one out whenever you experience a mood change. Notice what you were doing, where you were, what you were thinking, and ultimately how your thinking influenced your feelings.

THOUGHT RECORD

Situation (Describe the event without any thoughts or feelings, just pure description.)

Thoughts (Write what you thought in the situation.)

Emotions (Write how you felt—for example, sad, angry, anxious, disgusted, humiliated, ashamed.)

Below is an example of a completed thought record form. Remember Matthew from the introduction? He is a forty-one-year-old divorced male who is mainly concerned with the shape of his nose. In one of his cognitive therapy sessions, Matthew and his therapist examined Matthew's thoughts after a recent dinner party that he attended at a friend's house.

THOUGHT RECORD (SAMPLE)

Situation Met a friend's coworker and he was well dressed.

Thoughts

- *He probably thinks I'm boring.*

- *He's so much better looking than I am.*

- *I'm sure if we met again, he wouldn't give me the time of day.*

Emotions Disgust, sadness, impatience, anxiety

Hopefully, the "Identifying Automatic Thoughts" exercise helped you become more aware of your thoughts. Now that you know how to notice your thoughts, you're ready for the next step.

Step 2: Label Cognitive Distortions

The next step in cognitive therapy is to find a pattern in your negative thinking. Many individuals who experience anxiety or depression have certain styles of thinking and notice that a variety of situations bring up the same kinds of negative thought patterns. These negative patterns of thinking are called *cognitive distortions*. Take a look at the list below and try to place your thoughts into these categories. Some of these distortions do overlap, but there are differences. Don't be discouraged if you feel a particular thought falls into more than one category.

SOME COMMON COGNITIVE DISTORTIONS

Catastrophizing: You expect, even visualize, disaster. You notice or hear about a problem and start asking, "What if?" *What if tragedy strikes? What if it happens to me?*

Emotional reasoning: Your feelings guide the way you think, feel, and behave.

Filtering: You focus on the negative details while ignoring all the positive aspects of a situation.

Fortune telling: You make predictions about the future and assume them to be true.

Magnifying: You exaggerate the degree or intensity of a problem. You turn up the volume on anything bad, making it loud, large, and overwhelming.

Mind reading: Without their saying so, you believe you know what people feel and why they act the way they do. In particular, you feel you have certain knowledge of how people think and feel about you.

Overgeneralization: You reach a general conclusion based on a single incident or piece of evidence. You exaggerate the frequency of problems and use negative global labels, such as "I look horrible in that picture; therefore, I'm ugly."

Personalization: You assume that everything people do or say is some kind of reaction to you. You also compare yourself to others, trying to determine who is smarter, more competent, better looking, and so on.

Polarized thinking: Things are black or white, good or bad. You have to be perfect or you're a failure. There's no middle ground, no room for mistakes.

"Should" statements: You have a list of ironclad rules about how you and other people should act. For example, "People should return phone calls immediately" or "I should look good all the time." People who break the rules anger you, and you feel guilty when you violate the rules.

Don't be discouraged if you struggle with labeling your thoughts, since many of the categories sound similar and overlap. The main goal of thought records and identifying distortions is to recognize that your thoughts follow certain patterns. When you recognize the patterns, you can learn to think in a more flexible way. We want you to make conclusions based on the objective evidence around you rather than relying on your own pattern of negative thinking. Sessions with a therapist trained in cognitive therapy will help you master identifying and recognizing negative thought patterns.

Let's return to Matthew's thought record form (above). Using the list of cognitive distortions, we can label his first thought as mind reading and his third thought as fortune telling. Like Matthew, once you're able to identify the corresponding cognitive distortion, you'll be more aware of the way you think. Being aware of your style of thinking will allow you to catch yourself the next time you're mind reading or fortune telling. Once you've identified your thoughts and corresponding cognitive distortions, you can move on to the next step in cognitive therapy, which is to challenge your thoughts.

Step 3: Challenge Thoughts

Challenging thoughts is a challenging process! Here are some general rules about thoughts that most cognitive therapists teach their clients:

- Thoughts should not be mistaken for facts. A thought is just a mental experience, and having a thought doesn't make something the absolute truth.

- Thoughts are not dangerous or harmful; only behaviors can be dangerous or harmful.

- No matter how much you "feel" that something is true, it still may just be your perception of the situation.

Here are some techniques you can use to challenge your thoughts. They have been adapted from some well-known researchers in the field of cognitive therapy, including Aaron Beck, Judith Beck, Albert Ellis, and David Burns.

Use the Outside Observer Technique

Cognitive therapy requires you to take a step back from your thoughts and critically evaluate them from an outsider's perspective. Pretend for a few minutes that these thoughts belong to someone else. This may help you reduce the emotional experience of challenging them. If it were a friend or loved one expressing these thoughts and negative emotions, how might you help this person think logically and cope with the bad feelings? For example, imagine that you're anxious about attending your upcoming birthday party and are thinking of canceling it. What if your friend told you she wasn't going to have a party for herself because she felt too unattractive to be around people? What advice would you give her? Perhaps you'd tell her that her friends and family are more focused on celebrating her birthday than focused on her looks. They would enjoy the party because they care about her and love her as a person.

Apply the Double Standard Technique

When you're thinking negatively about yourself or your actions, ask yourself how you'd view your friend or loved one in the same situation. Would you be as critical of your friend as you are of yourself, or would you be more supportive, encouraging, and understanding? The double standard suggests that you have unrealistic standards for yourself and more fair/realistic standards for others. For example, if you come home from a first date and are angry with yourself for not being talkative or interesting enough, imagine what you would say to a friend in the same situation. You might tell her that she did the best she could. First dates can be awkward and difficult for even the most socially skilled. So, try being fairer in your judgments of yourself.

Try the Survey Others Technique

Do a real or imaginary survey and find out if your thoughts or beliefs are reasonable and realistic. Reexamine your conclusions if you find that others do not think the same way. For example, if you believe that happiness can only be achieved by looking good, ask others how they value appearance and looks.

Apply the Scientific Method

Another effective approach is to pretend you're a scientist and your thoughts are just hypotheses. A *hypothesis* (for those of you rusty on your middle school science) is simply an educated guess. A hypothesis is open to being accepted or rejected based on evidence. In science, that usually means collecting some kind of data and then reviewing whether the evidence proves or rejects the hypothesis. Over time and years of research, a hypothesis may become an accepted theory and eventually a "law of nature." But until then, most hypotheses are not readily accepted without sufficient evidence. So, if you apply this principle to cognitive therapy, your thoughts and perceptions about situations are just hypotheses. Given this, the first step in challenging thoughts using the scientific method is to ask yourself, *Where's the evidence to support or reject this thought?* Here's a list of questions to ask when you challenge your thoughts:

- Where is the evidence?

- How likely is this to occur?

- How feasible is it?

- Why must I be accepted?

- Is it possible for me to be accepted by everyone?

- Even if people accept me, is it possible for them to approve of or accept me all the time?

- What is the disastrous consequence, if any, and can I cope with it?

- If my thought is true, is it the end of the world?

- What makes me think I can't handle it?

Another more active way to apply the scientific method is to get out there and actually gather the data. For example, imagine that one of your beliefs is that people stare at your face and don't treat you well because of it. One way to gather data is to spend a couple of hours in the mall with a pen and paper and make observations. Count how many people stopped to stare at you, and, conversely, count how many people walked by without appearing to take special notice. Counting the second part of that exercise is especially important, because many people with BDD are more obser-vant of the negative experiences than they are of the neutral or positive experiences. If you're brave, the next step in the exercise might be to make some social contact with a few shoppers and salespeople and see how they react to you. Ask a salesperson for help locating an item, ask another shopper if he knows where a particular store is, or start a friendly conversa-tion with someone while in line at the food court. Notice how others treat you. Go home and count the data. Does this one experience support or not support your initial hypothesis?

Step 4: Find Your Global Thinking Pattern

Now that you've learned to identify, label, and challenge your thoughts, the next step is to see the global pattern in your thinking style. Judith Beck reports that there are two deeper levels of our thoughts: intermediate and core beliefs. Let's look first at intermediate beliefs.

Intermediate Beliefs

Intermediate beliefs are underlying and rigid assumptions. Here is a list of common intermediate beliefs expressed by our BDD clients:

- I can't be happy until my appearance improves.

- Nothing is more important than appearance.

- I'll always be alone in life unless my appearance improves.

- Achieving physical perfection is a reasonable goal.

Intermediate beliefs, as we said above, are underlying and rigid assumptions; they come from core beliefs, which we'll explore more thoroughly below. Both intermediate and core beliefs are the "deeper level" beliefs, whereas automatic thoughts are our immediate responses to particular situations. Let's go back to our example of Matthew from earlier in this chapter. Matthew went to a dinner party and after his conversation with someone, his automatic thoughts were *He probably thinks I'm boring, He's so much better looking than me,* and *I'm sure if we met again, he wouldn't give me the time of day.* Matthew's intermediate beliefs might be *I'm not good enough* and *People don't like me.* His core belief might be *I'm inadequate.*

Core Beliefs

Core beliefs, according to Judith Beck, are our fundamental beliefs about ourselves, our world, and others. They develop early in childhood and continue to influence how we view things, even if evidence doesn't support it. Here are some examples of core beliefs:

- The world isn't safe.

- People can't be trusted.

- I'm inadequate.

- I'm worthless.

- There's something defective about me.

- I'm a good person.

- People are essentially good.

Our automatic and intermediate thoughts are a reflection of these core beliefs. Let's see how to identify automatic, intermediate, and core beliefs using the experience of a client named Ben.

Ben is a twenty-five-year-old with a long history of depression. He's been in therapy for the past month and is already familiar with the basics of cognitive therapy. He was late to work yesterday because he spent five extra minutes choosing his shirt and then hit traffic on his commute. He felt very frustrated and angry at himself. His automatic thoughts were (1) *My boss will be so angry with me*, (2) *He'll think I'm an unreliable employee and then I'm never going to get a raise*, and (3) *I can't do anything right lately*. The best way for Ben to determine what his intermediate thoughts and core beliefs are to use the downward arrow technique.

USE THE DOWNWARD ARROW TECHNIQUE

The downward arrow technique guides you to core beliefs that underlie more surface-level automatic thoughts. For each of your automatic thoughts, ask yourself, "Then what?" Ask that question over and over until you hit a core belief. You'll know you've hit a core belief when you can't ask yourself "Then what?" any further. Let's use Ben's first thought to demonstrate:

My boss will be so angry at me. (Then what?)

That means he might question my competence. (Then what?)

Then he might fire me. (Then what?)

↓

Then I won't be able to support myself, and I'll have to move back in with my parents. (Then what?)

↓

That means I'm a failure and can't do anything right!

In Ben's case, his core belief was *I'm a failure.* See if you can identify your core beliefs.

Now that you have learned to challenge and modify your intermediate and core beliefs, let's examine more closely your beliefs about the importance of appearance.

TARGET YOUR VALUE OF APPEARANCE

In chapter 2, we reviewed how early life experiences and modeling contributed to your beliefs about your appearance and the importance of appearance. Try this exercise to challenge the importance and value you place on appearance and to understand how your mood influences your beliefs and values about appearance.

EXERCISE: Challenging Your Value of Appearance

On two different days, reflect on the questions below. First, choose a day when your mood is reasonably good, and then choose a day when you struggle with your BDD. Answer the questions as honestly as you can.

- Why can't looks just be one aspect of my life?

- Am I a bad person overall just based on appearance alone?

- If I choose to focus only on one aspect of myself as a person, why does it have to be looks? Can I choose to focus on something else, such as intelligence, personality, or career achievement?

- Why do I have to be the most attractive person in the room? If others are good looking, does that take away from my appearance?

- Just because there's someone whose (body part of concern) is better looking than mine, does that make mine more unattractive?

- If I don't look perfect, then am I ugly?

- Even if my body part of concern may not be perfect, does that mean I'm unattractive overall?

- Does my overall happiness have to be based on looking good?

- Is physical perfection both possible and desirable?

Did you answer the questions differently based on your mood? This suggests a few important things. On days in which your thoughts are more rational, you're less negative in your judgments about yourself and how much you value appearance. Aim for a more balanced view of appearance and its importance in your life. Take action. Match your daily activities with your balanced view of appearance. Act as if appearance is less important in your life. How would you spend a day if this was the case? Would you take a drive in a convertible and forget about your hair looking frizzy and windblown? Would you spend a day at the beach enjoying the sun and water? In chapter 8, you'll learn more strategies to focus on other life values. This will help you with your BDD by shifting your primary focus off of the importance of appearance in your life.

Overvalued Ideation

So, you've read most of this chapter, and if you've tried all of these techniques without much benefit, you may be asking yourself, *What now?* Cognitive therapy takes time to process, practice, and master. Perhaps your lack of progress will simply be solved by practicing these techniques for a longer time. Many people with BDD have strong convictions and beliefs that psychologists call "overvalued ideation." A high OVI suggests that you hold strongly to beliefs about your appearance and the value and importance of appearance. In this case, cognitive therapy may take more practice and time to benefit you.

In order to test your OVI level, complete the following questionnaire, the Overvalued Ideas Scale, which some colleagues and I (Fugen Neziroglu) developed.

OVERVALUED IDEAS SCALE

Please think about the body part that causes you the most distress and identify your belief about this body part. (Here are some examples of BDD beliefs: *I will never be happy unless my hair looks good; No one will be attracted to me because of the size of my nose; I am flawed as a person because of my appearance.*)

Describe the main belief below:

_____

_____

_____

_____

Rate all the following categories based on this belief as you've experienced it in the past week, including today. Each category (except #7) asks three questions. You may use all three questions to help you provide an accurate answer.

1. STRENGTH OF BELIEF

How strongly do you believe that this belief is true?

How certain/convinced are you that this belief is true?

Can your belief be "shaken" if it is challenged by you or someone else?

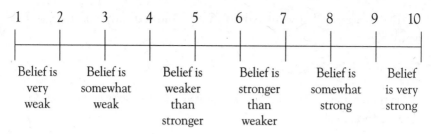

| 1 | 2 | 3 | 4 | 5 | 6 | 7 | 8 | 9 | 10 |

Belief is very weak — Belief is somewhat weak — Belief is weaker than stronger — Belief is stronger than weaker — Belief is somewhat strong — Belief is very strong

("Very weak" to "very strong" refers to the possibility of the belief being true—that is, "very weak" means that it's minimally possible that it's true; "very strong" means it's extremely possible that it's true.)

Rating Item 1: _____

2. REASONABLENESS OF BELIEF

How reasonable is your belief?

Is your belief justified or rational?

Is the belief logical or does it seem reasonable?

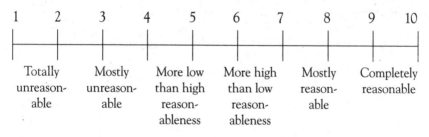

| 1 | 2 | 3 | 4 | 5 | 6 | 7 | 8 | 9 | 10 |

Totally unreasonable — Mostly unreasonable — More low than high reasonableness — More high than low reasonableness — Mostly reasonable — Completely reasonable

Rating Item 2: _____

3. LOWEST STRENGTH OF BELIEF

In the last week, what would you say was the lowest rating of strength for your belief?

How weak did your belief become in the last week?

Were there times in the past week that you doubted your belief, even for a fleeting moment?

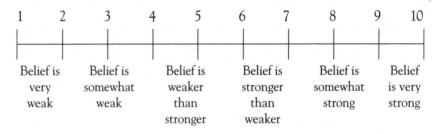

Rating Item 3: _____

4. HIGHEST STRENGTH OF BELIEF

In the last week, what was your highest rating of strength for your belief?

How strong did your belief become in the last week?

How certain/convinced were you about your belief in the past week?

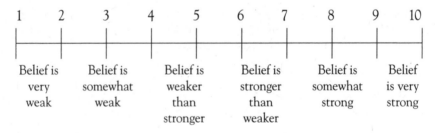

Rating Item 4: _____

5. ACCURACY OF BELIEF

How accurate is your belief?

How correct is your belief?

To what degree is your belief erroneous?

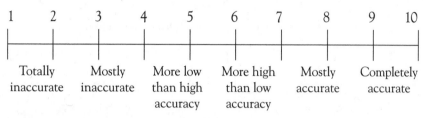

| 1 | 2 | 3 | 4 | 5 | 6 | 7 | 8 | 9 | 10 |

Totally inaccurate · Mostly inaccurate · More low than high accuracy · More high than low accuracy · Mostly accurate · Completely accurate

Rating Item 5: _____

6. EXTENT OF ADHERENCE BY OTHERS

How likely is it that others in the general population (in your community, state, country, and so on) have the same belief?

How strongly do these others agree with your belief?

To what extent do these others share your belief?

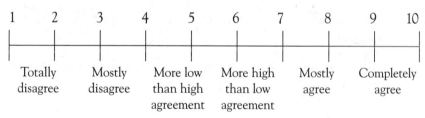

| 1 | 2 | 3 | 4 | 5 | 6 | 7 | 8 | 9 | 10 |

Totally disagree · Mostly disagree · More low than high agreement · More high than low agreement · Mostly agree · Completely agree

Rating Item 6: _____

7. ATTRIBUTION OF DIFFERING VIEWS BY OTHERS

Do others share the same belief as you? Yes _____ No _____

If you answer yes, go to 7a; if you answer no, go to 7b.

7a. VIEW OTHERS AS POSSESSING SAME BELIEF

Since you think others agree with your belief, do you think they are as knowledgeable as you about this belief?

To what extent do you believe others are as knowledgeable about the belief as you are?

Do you believe others have as much information as you about this belief?

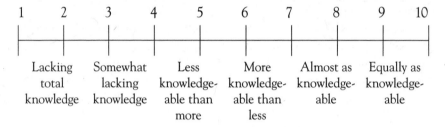

Rating Item 7a: _____

7b. VIEW OTHERS AS HOLDING DIFFERING BELIEF

Since you think others disagree with you, do you think they are less knowledgeable than you about this belief?

To what extent do you believe others are less knowledgeable about the belief than you are?

Do you believe others have less information than you about this belief?

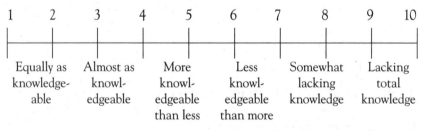

Rating Item 7b: _____

8. EFFECTIVENESS OF COMPULSIONS

How effective are your compulsions/ritualistic behaviors in preventing negative consequences other than anxiety?

Are your compulsions of any value in stopping the feared outcome?

Is it possible that your compulsions may not help prevent the negative outcomes?

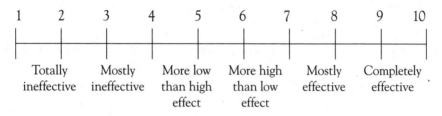

Totally ineffective	Mostly ineffective	More low than high effect	More high than low effect	Mostly effective	Completely effective

Rating Item 8: _____

9. INSIGHT

To what extent do you think that your disorder has caused you to have this belief?

How probable is it that your beliefs are due to psychological or psychiatric reasons?

Do you think that your belief is due to a disorder?

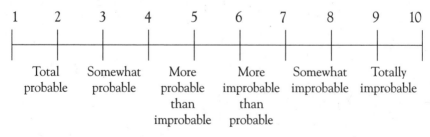

Total probable	Somewhat probable	More probable than improbable	More improbable than probable	Somewhat improbable	Totally improbable

Rating Item 9: _____

10. STRENGTH OF RESISTANCE

How much energy do you put into rejecting your belief?

How strongly do you try to change your belief?

Do you attempt to resist your belief?

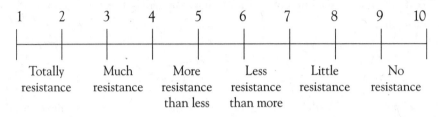

| 1 | 2 | 3 | 4 | 5 | 6 | 7 | 8 | 9 | 10 |

Totally resistance   Much resistance   More resistance than less   Less resistance than more   Little resistance   No resistance

Rating Item 10: _____

You can now add up the scores in the ten categories and divide it by ten. Any number 6 or higher indicates that you have high overvalued ideas, meaning you have strong conviction in your beliefs. They are therefore more difficult to change; however, they are changeable.

(Adapted from Overvalued Ideas Scale by Fugen A. Neziroglu, Jose A. Yaryura-Tobias, Dean R. McKay, Kevin Stevens, and John Todaro. Copyright Fugen A. Neziroglu 1998. Used by permission.)

In this chapter, you learned that by identifying your thoughts and challenging them, you can change your feelings. Perhaps you're still skeptical because you're so familiar with our society's preference for skinny and attractive people. You might even cite Malcolm Gladwell who, in his book *Blink*, reveals that CEOs of Fortune 500 companies are on average three inches taller than the average American male. So, given a fact like that, how can we possibly suggest that changing your thoughts is the answer? That doesn't seem to make sense when the rest of society hasn't changed their thoughts about what is considered attractive, does it?

We do take this concern seriously and acknowledge that we sometimes ask our clients to rise above society's standard. On the other hand, have you noticed that what the data says doesn't always match real people? Do you have a friend who suffers from a weight problem yet has a great job and a great husband? Do you know of a couple in which the woman is more attractive than the man? Can you think of celebrities who may not necessarily fit the typical Hollywood standard? We encourage you to continue collecting this type of data. You'll notice that there are a number of exceptions to the rule. So is it possible to live a productive and happy life and place less importance on appearance? You know our answer to that question—a definite yes!

In this chapter, you've learned how to modify your thoughts by using techniques to challenge them. Hopefully, you've begun to change some of your BDD thoughts. The next step in fighting your BDD is to directly change your daily actions. The next chapter will show you how to do that.

6

Behavior Therapy

Using Exposure and Response Prevention

Congratulations on progressing through the previous chapter. We encourage you to continue actively using cognitive therapy skills as you move forward in the book. Now that you've learned ways to balance thoughts and emotions, this chapter will help you change the daily routines and behaviors that may cause stress. Perhaps you check your appearance in the mirror many times in a day, struggle with getting dressed in the mornings, are careful where you go and the time of day when you go out, are conscious about how you sit, or limit your activities more than you would like. These are some of the behaviors we hope to tackle with you using the next component of treatment, which is called "behavior therapy."

What Is Behavior Therapy?

Behavior therapy is a type of treatment aimed at understanding and changing unwanted behaviors. It consists of several different techniques that can be applied to many situations and problems. There are specific behavioral techniques to help students develop better study skills, to help parents use effective discipline, to help smokers quit smoking, and to help people suffering from anxiety and depression learn to overcome their illness. The type of behavior therapy you'll learn to use in this chapter is called *exposure and response prevention*, or ERP, as we'll call it for the remainder of this book. ERP, in a nutshell, is based on the concept that when you face your fears and do not engage in safety behaviors that help reduce anxiety, you ultimately will not be fearful. It's a straightforward and commonsense strategy for overcoming fears. If you had a friend with a phobia of the water, what advice would you offer? You don't need years of formal psychology training to suggest he should probably overcome his fear by taking swimming lessons or start going into the pool very gradually and see that nothing bad happens.

These are the kinds of strategies we'll suggest in this chapter. We'll help you identify the situations and activities that currently cause you a lot of discomfort and the ones that you currently avoid. We know that sounds like a terribly difficult task. And you're right! It is a difficult task, but we've witnessed hundreds of our clients overcome their fears by using these techniques. We've seen them triumph over their obstacles and experience immense relief at being able to carry out their daily lives without their previous level of suffering. So as you read on, we encourage you to take some risks and give behavior therapy a try.

The History and Development of Behavior Therapy

Behavior therapy for anxiety disorders was a true revolution in the field of psychology. Our field took an important step forward in joining the other sciences when we stepped into a laboratory and began using scientific methods to develop treatments. Early therapy, such as Sigmund Freud's psychoanalytic theory and treatment, was based mainly on his observations of the clients he treated. The theories were not, however, tested in laboratory studies. Much of the early writings in psychological therapy were detailed case descriptions of clients, and conclusions were drawn from a handful of situations.

During the same time that Freud published his papers on psychoanalysis, however, a change in the field of psychological therapy occurred. Scientists began systematically studying a variety of behaviors and emotions. Of interest to us, of course, was the research being conducted on how humans develop anxiety, phobias, and fears. John B. Watson conducted one of the most famous experiments in psychology by demonstrating that humans could learn to become fearful of certain objects or situations through life experiences. Naturally, scientists asked themselves this question: if anxiety can be learned, can it be "unlearned?"

That's exactly what was demonstrated in animal experiments from the 1940s to the 1960s. Frightened animals were taught to be less fearful by being exposed gradually to the situation they feared. Then in 1966, Victor Meyer applied these techniques for people suffering from OCD. He found that if people were exposed to their feared situations for a prolonged time and were not allowed to avoid, escape, or perform their rituals, they became less afraid. From that point forward, the studies in and publications about behavior therapy in OCD treatment exploded. These techniques were found to be so effective for OCD that they were gradually tested and found effective for other conditions, including BDD of course!

In summary, ERP is a type of behavior therapy used for OCD, BDD, and other similar conditions. Based on all the early research, both with animals and with humans, we can confidently say that it's an extremely effective method of improving the lives of people who suffer from BDD.

How Can I Use Exposure and Response Prevention for BDD?

Since BDD isn't technically a fear or phobia, how might ERP be applied to BDD? As you have read in earlier chapters, BDD is essentially a first cousin to OCD. People with BDD think about their appearance for many hours a day and also engage in ritual behaviors to improve, check, or camouflage their appearance. It's also common for people with BDD to avoid certain situations that cause anxiety or discomfort. ERP can be a very useful tool to help people gradually face (exposure) the uncomfortable situations while preventing the ritual behaviors (camouflaging, checking). For example, remember Ana, whom you met in the beginning of the book? She was an eighteen-year-old concerned about skin redness and acne. Some of Ana's in-session ERP exercises consisted of trips to brightly lit stores and crowded places while gradually reducing her rituals—use of skin products, hand washing, and other ritual behaviors. The therapist started out with helping Ana face the least difficult situations and gradually worked up to more challenging exercises.

Preparing for ERP: Common Worries

We understand if you're experiencing some anxiety or doubt about the treatment. Many of our clients have expressed concerns as well. We'd like to address some of these concerns in the hope that you'll feel comfortable with the treatment.

"I don't want to be forced to face my fears." Many people have heard or read about behavior therapy and fear that the therapist will insist on certain exercises. But this is far from the truth. A well-trained behavioral therapist allows the client to be an equal partner in the development of a treatment plan. Many clients we've treated decided not to engage in the behavioral strategies at first. If you decide you're not ready for this phase of treatment once you finish reading this chapter, we suggest you go back and reread the chapter on cognitive therapy and practice those skills, and then read chapter 8 on acceptance and commitment therapy. The strategies in chapter 8 are geared especially for people who experience doubt about therapy.

"I don't avoid many things; I just feel sad and upset every day." If you're someone who continues to engage in your daily life even though it causes you anxiety, sadness, or frustration, you may wonder how ERP would work for you. Even if you don't avoid many situations, perhaps you make certain accommodations as a result of your concern about your appearance. For example, do you have a very specific process for doing your hair in the morning and can't go out until it looks a certain way? Or do you feel compelled to spend time on social networking websites comparing your appearance to others? Do these things lead to more frustration and anxiety? Do these things make you late to various events? These are some of the behaviors that ERP can help change.

"I won't be able to tolerate the anxiety." This is probably the most common concern of the people we've treated. They tell us, "I can't do it! It's just too hard!" We're actually happy that our clients express this concern. It gives us the opportunity to explain how ERP can work so effectively. ERP, like exercise, gradually builds "muscles." The first exposures leave you quite sore afterward, but as you practice, your tolerance and strength improve. When our clients look back on their initial sessions, they wonder why those "small" exercises bothered them at all. Then they're amazed at the things they're able to do. Many say things like this: "If you'd asked me six months ago if I could go to a party without my hat on, I would have said you were nuts!" This decrease in anxiety with repeated practice is called habituation, and it is one of the essential processes of the therapy.

"What's the point; it won't change how I feel about my looks." We admit that this is a tough concern to answer. For some people, body image takes a lot longer to change than thoughts and emotions. It may sound odd, but it is possible to improve your daily life even if you still believe your appearance is flawed. Your body image, after all, took years to develop and is a core part of what you value and who you are. The cognitive and behavioral strategies can significantly improve your daily activities as well as help shift your beliefs. Your core body image may take a bit longer to change; you may need more experiences to help you improve how you view your body. The more you interact in the world, socialize, and achieve your short- and long-term goals, the more positive experiences you will have. These positive experiences add up and over time help you reexamine some of your core beliefs. So, don't throw in the towel yet. Continue on with these strategies.

Building a Hierarchy

So, if you're ready to take action and try some of these techniques, the first step is to build a list of anxiety-causing situations and behaviors in your daily life. This list is formally called a "hierarchy." It's the tool you'll use to design and carry out exposure exercises. A *hierarchy* is put in order based on the level of anxiety particular situations or behaviors create. Typically, each item on the list is assigned a number on a scale of 1 to 100 or 1 to 10, with higher numbers indicating higher anxiety levels.

Here are two examples of hierarchies from our case studies:

Ana's Hierarchy for Skin Imperfections	Keith's Hierarchy for Muscularity
100 Going out to dinner on a Friday night without makeup	100 Skipping the gym and then going out with friends
95 Going to class without makeup and sitting up front	
90 Going to bed without washing face	90 Skipping the gym
80 Going to class without makeup and sitting in the back	
80 Touching face after touching public doorknobs	80 Hugging someone
70 Eating chocolate or french fries	70 Eating a nonprotein meal
60 Coming to a therapy appointment without makeup	60 Not weighing self or not measuring biceps or quadriceps
50 Reading a newspaper and then touching face	50 Skipping one set of arm or leg exercises at the gym
40 Leaving home without checking face in the mirror	40 Sitting near someone on the train
30 Sitting in therapy session without makeup	30 Wearing a form-fitting shirt
20 Shaking hands with someone and then touching face	

It can be difficult to sit down with a piece of paper and just start building a hierarchy. We find that the exercise below is very useful in the beginning phase of treatment. Now that you're familiar with hierarchies, try this exercise to help you determine your own list.

EXERCISE: A Typical Day

Imagine a typical day in your life. Imagine yourself going through every step of your day. Include all of the tiny details, including how you wake up, how and when you brush your teeth, and so on. As you imagine each of these activities, ask yourself, *Does BDD influence how I do this?*

Once you've imagined your day, go through an actual day. You may find it helpful to jot down other actions you may have missed when you imagined your day. Your list may look something like this:

- Woke up to alarm and first thought was *Ugh, another day I have to face the mirror*

- Went to bathroom mirror to check if acne had changed

- Showered and spent five extra minutes using skin-cleansing soap

- Got dressed and took thirty minutes to put on makeup

- Left home and checked reflection in car mirror while stuck in traffic

- Early meeting at work—sat near the door to avoid being near people

- At lunch, washed hands after touching dirty chairs and table

A hierarchy based on this list might look like this:

- Skip the morning mirror check

- Wash face only once in shower

- Walk into office without checking appearance

- Sit next to boss in the meeting

- Touch face after touching chair in restaurant

Once you have a list of situations from a typical day, think of things you've wanted to do but couldn't because of your anxiety or discomfort.

Think of activities you used to do many months or years ago. Have you avoided going out to dinner? Have you avoided fancy restaurants? Did you stop going to the gym? Include these activities in your hierarchy. Your hierarchy should consist of both types of situations: ones you avoid and ones you engage in with BDD behaviors.

You are almost there! The last step in building a hierarchy is to reorder this list based on the amount of anxiety it causes you. One method we find useful is to write each of these situations on a separate index card and then shuffle them around until they're in "anxiety order," from least to most anxiety. This is sometimes more challenging than it might initially seem. Many people report that all of these situations are a 100. We encourage you to assign a value of 100 only to the most difficult and "worst" situation you can imagine. If everything is a 100, it won't seem possible to start ERP. Another technique is to reexamine some of the items and break them down into smaller steps. For example, instead of just listing "going out to dinner," you might want to have separate exercises for "going out to dinner on a date," "going out to dinner where no one knows me," "going to dinner where I'm likely to run into people I know," and "going out to dinner with friends on a Friday night." Each of these exercises might create different levels of anxiety for you.

Another important concept in ERP is measuring your anxiety or distress level during the actual exposure exercise. This distress level is referred to as a "SUDS" level by cognitive behavioral therapists. *SUDS* stands for *subjective units of distress scale.* In essence, this refers to how anxious you feel throughout the exposure exercise. In order for exposure to be effective, we aim for a 70 percent reduction in your SUDS level from the beginning to the end of an exercise. So, if you're doing an exposure walking around a store with your hair in a ponytail and your initial SUDS is a 100, you should try to remain in the store until you feel your anxiety level decrease to a 30.

Hopefully, your hierarchy is somewhat complete. Don't worry if it's not perfect. A hierarchy is not written in stone. In fact, we edit hierarchies quite often. As you progress through the exercises, certain things may not even bother you anymore and you'll learn more about your BDD than you initially realized.

Early Steps in ERP

Once you've built your hierarchy, we suggest that you put it aside for a little while. Why? Do you remember that ERP has two parts? Exposure *and* response prevention. In order for behavior therapy to be the most effective, both parts are needed—that is, you need to face fearful situations like those on your hierarchy list (exposure) while not engaging in your rituals (response prevention). So, instead of diving right into the exposure part of ERP, we'd first like you to spend some time reducing your rituals. This may seem confusing since many of the items on your hierarchy include both components, such as going out to dinner without a hat or makeup on. You may be asking yourself, *Won't I be doing exposure if I decrease my makeup use and continue with my daily life?* Yes, you're correct that many of your exposure exercises ask you to refrain from your rituals. Although there's overlap in ERP exercises, it's sometimes simpler to separate the components—and to begin working with your rituals. There also might be other rituals not listed on your hierarchy. In addition, it may take some preparation and practice to start reducing your rituals.

For this reason, we first ask the people we treat to keep a daily list of their rituals and then slowly decrease them in a gradual and systematic way. This makes the exposure exercises significantly easier to do. So this is what we're asking of you, too. The exercise below will help you begin to reduce your rituals.

EXERCISE: Ritual Reduction

In chapter 1, you listed your rituals in the exercise called "Symptoms Checklist." Take out that list now and review it. Does it still apply to you? Can you think of other ways in which you hide, change, improve, or check your appearance daily?

For each of your rituals, such as mirror checking, excessive exercise, or styling your hair, keep a three-day log of how often and for how long you do it. You can use the log below by making photocopies or transcribing it into your notebook. Be sure to include the date and time, where you were, how long you did the ritual, why you did the ritual, and how you felt during the ritual and afterward. (You can use the log below—both for your three-day record and also when you choose a ritual that you want to do less frequently.)

RITUAL LOG

Date	Time	Where was I?	How long did I do the ritual?	Why did I do the ritual?	How did I feel during the ritual?	How did I feel after the ritual?

After you have completed your log, choose one ritual and try to cut it down in small stages or cut out one aspect of it. For example, if you mirror checked about twenty times a day, try to cut it down to fifteen times a day. Another example: if you mirror check in various places but find that the one most difficult to give up is your bathroom mirror and the easiest to give up is your pocket mirror, then start with giving up the latter. We recognize that you won't be able to just stop your rituals in a week, but any decrease in the amount and number of rituals will help you move forward in ERP.

Coping with Mirror Checking

Since mirror checking is the most common and sometimes the hardest ritual to break, here are some tips and techniques to reduce it. Occasionally people with BDD avoid mirrors, but approximately 90 percent mirror check. Mirrors and reflected surfaces are found everywhere, and since it only takes a second to check your reflection, how do you ignore the urge to take a quick peek? The first step is to be aware of how often and under what circumstances you mirror check. There might be times in a day that it's become such an automatic habit that you don't even realize you're doing it. Keeping a log of your checking increases your awareness of it. In your log, include your thoughts and motivation for checking, how you feel while you're checking, and the consequence to your emotions as a result of checking—that is, how do you feel afterward?

Here are the most common reasons people with BDD mirror check:

- Checking to see if appearance changed

- Checking to see if appearance looks different in different mirrors

- Improving and fixing appearance by brushing hair or applying more cosmetic products

- Using strategies to hide or camouflage appearance

- Comparing reflection with a mental image or with an ideal image

- Checking mirror as a result of a trigger in the immediate environment, such as being near a very attractive person

- Attaching a habit to certain activities (for example, while brushing your teeth) or times of the day

- Experimenting with certain poses, facial expressions, hairstyles, or makeup application

- Seeking comfort

- Having something to do at the end of the night

Use the log from the previous exercise. At the top of the log, write your reason for mirror checking from the above list. Once you have kept a log, try to systematically eliminate or decrease the checking either by trigger type or the amount of time you check. Using cognitive therapy to challenge your thoughts would be extremely helpful as well.

If the urge to resist is very strong, it might be beneficial to initially remove or cover some of the mirrors in your environment. If you have small makeup or magnifying mirrors in your bedroom, it would be wise to remove them temporarily. Ask a family member to hold them for you. If you need them for cosmetic reasons, such as applying makeup or putting on contact lenses, borrow them just to complete the necessary tasks. Some people simply covered their bathroom vanity mirrors. We recognize that mirrors are a part of daily life, but hiding them in the initial stages of treatment can help you gain control of the checking. Once you've achieved some level of control, try reintroducing some of the mirrors in your house. Other techniques include setting a timer to limit the amount of mirror time and delaying the urge to check one minute at a time. Usage of mirrors should be limited to normal daily activities where the average person uses a mirror—that is, shaving, putting on makeup, taking off makeup. Aim for average!

Another technique to limit mirror checking is to set some ground rules for checking. Try some of these suggested rules:

- "I will not check after 8 p.m. since it prevents me from sleeping."

- "I will not check until after I shower because 99.9 percent of people don't like how they look first thing in the morning."

- "I will not check while driving because it's dangerous."

- "I will not check when I'm home for the night; what's the point of impressing my dog?"

Sometimes you may need to remind yourself of the ground rules that you've set. We suggest that you take these rules—as well as some self-affirming statements like "I can overcome BDD!"—write them on index cards, and tape them up next to your mirror. This way you'll be more likely to follow through.

Tips for Doing Exposure Exercises

After you've decreased your rituals as much as you possibly can, you're ready to tackle the hierarchy you initially created. Here are some suggestions to help you successfully do exposure:

Find a partner. It can be easier to carry out challenging tasks in life using the buddy system. Ideally, cognitive behavioral therapists make the best coaches, but if you're not currently in therapy, think of someone in your life who is trustworthy and has a positive outlook. If you're in a support group, then perhaps you can partner up with another member. Since just a few BDD support groups exist, it's unlikely that there's one in your area—but do check, just in case there is. If there isn't a BDD support group near you, consider joining a support group for anxiety, OCD, improving body image, depression, or social anxiety. These may not be an exact fit, but they might help you connect with others who suffer in similar ways.

Start at the bottom. On your hierarchy list, choose your lowest anxiety item first. Don't skip ahead to try exercises that are too difficult. Occasionally this works for people who have a mild level of BDD. As a general rule, though, it's prudent to start slowly and build up your skills before progressing to the really challenging exercises. We don't want you to feel hopeless or discouraged that you can't tolerate the therapy, and going too quickly can easily become overwhelming.

Repeat until bored. We often joke that our goal in providing ERP therapy is to create boredom. We want our clients to be bored doing exposures!

Boredom is the opposite of anxiety and suggests the person has gotten used to the feared situation. This process of decreasing anxiety through repeated exposure is called habituation. Repeat your exposure exercises over and over until you experience minimal anxiety. Once you have achieved that level, move on to the next item on your list.

Consider this an endurance test. As we mentioned before, research consistently shows that exposure is effective when people experience a reduction in anxiety during the actual exposure. In an ideal situation, we aim for a 70 percent reduction in anxiety from the start to finish of any exposure exercise; accomplishing this takes time. When you do your exposure exercises, plan to stay in the situation as long as possible. If you're fearful of engaging in conversations with strangers at a close range, then plan to go to the mall for a couple of hours and go to more than one store to interact with others. We suggest you don't just speak to one person and then leave. This can sometimes make you feel more rather than less anxious. Reducing anxiety levels takes time, so stick with it. If you only reduced your anxiety level by 20 percent even though you stayed in the situation for a long time period, then you might need to repeat that particular exercise multiple times until you become accustomed to that situation.

Be a good record keeper. One way to recognize that you're progressing and improving is to look back and see how you did in past exposure exercises. Use a sheet similar to the one below every time you do an exposure:

EXPOSURE LOG

Exposure exercise: Sitting at coffee shop without hat

Length of Exposure: 1½ hours

Date: October 10, 2012

Beginning SUDS (subjective units of distress): 100

Ending SUDS: 30

Time to Achieve Lowest SUDS: 1 hour

Perhaps when you do this same exposure a week later, you notice that it only takes about thirty minutes for your anxiety to reduce from 100 to 30. A week after that you might notice that your beginning anxiety level is a 70 rather than 100! This will give you the hard evidence that ERP is working for you. Actually, you should go back every so often and practice older hierarchy items that you've already mastered. The more practice, the better. That's the best way to achieve good, lasting, and quick recovery.

EXERCISE: Let's Go!

Even though you've developed your own hierarchy of uncomfortable situations, there are universal situations most people with BDD would prefer to avoid. After you've proceeded through your own individual hierarchy, try these field trip exercises for "extra credit." Each of these exercises is broken down into three levels based on difficulty. If you're unsure of which to do, start with the "easiest" item and then move on to those that are more difficult for you.

LET'S GO SHOPPING

If you're concerned about being in big public places or interacting with strangers, try these:

Easiest: Shop at a superstore like Target or Walmart at night. Stay for at least twenty minutes and stand in line to purchase something.

Moderate: Go to a department store and talk to salespeople at the perfume counter.

Difficult: Shop at an exclusive boutique where salespeople typically engage in more lengthy conversations with you and make suggestions on items. Or pretend you're shopping for a new car and go to a car dealership and spend time speaking to a salesperson.

LET'S GET PAMPERED

If you're uncomfortable with others touching your body, try these:

Easiest: Schedule a manicure. (Men can get one, too.) Find a salon that caters to both genders and schedule an appointment during a quiet time. Usually late mornings during the middle of the week are the safest.

Moderate: Schedule a pedicure. (Men can get pedicures, too.)

Difficult: Schedule a full-body massage.

LET'S NETWORK

If you're uncomfortable with others seeing photographs of you, try these:

Easiest: Post a photo of yourself on a social networking website. If that's too difficult, perhaps you can start by posting a group photo where you are blurry or in the background.

Moderate: Add a photo of yourself alone and/or add of photo of yourself that isn't "perfect," such as a windblown beach shot or a candid shot.

Difficult: Find a goofy photo of yourself and post it—perhaps one in which you're making a silly face or dressed in a costume for Halloween.

LET'S VIDEOCHAT

If you're uncomfortable with videos, photos, or being on a screen in general, try these:

Easiest: Videochat with a family member like your aunt or grandmother.

Moderate: Videochat with a friend. If you must, keep the lights low and then gradually brighten the room.

Difficult: Videochat with someone you're romantically interested in or videochat without camouflaging your body part of concern. Or videochat in your pajamas!

LET'S STRIKE A POSE

If you're uncomfortable posing for photographs, try these:

Easiest: Ask a family member to take a photo or short video of you.

Moderate: Allow friends to take photos of you at a formal party or event.

Difficult: Schedule a photo shoot at a portrait studio or with a professional photographer.

LET'S GET NAKED

If you're self-conscious being naked even when you're alone, try these:

Easiest: Before you jump in the shower, turn the lights low in the bathroom and stand there for a few minutes.

Moderate: Walk around your bedroom naked while cleaning up for a few minutes.

Difficult: Spend an extended amount of time without clothes on at home.

LET'S GET SWEATY

If you're uncomfortable being sweaty or are concerned with appearing sloppy, try these:

Easiest: Go to a gym and work out during the late morning when it's quiet.

Moderate: Go to a gym and, after your workout, stop at the supermarket and shop.

Difficult: Go to the gym at a very crowded time (between 6 p.m. and 8 p.m. is a popular time) and work out where the serious weightlifters hang out.

LET'S GET A MAKEOVER

If having others examine your face up close makes you uncomfortable, try these:

Easiest: Go to a cosmetic store and ask a salesperson for advice on a lipstick color. For males, go to a department store and request help choosing an aftershave for sensitive skin.

Moderate: Go to a cosmetics store or department store makeup counter and ask a salesperson to apply a few lipstick colors. Or go to a counter that sells skin-cleansing or skin-moisturizing products and ask a salesperson to suggest products based on your skin type.

Difficult: Schedule an entire makeup application. Some cosmetic companies at department stores will charge you and others will not. For males, tell the salesperson that you've been told that there's a good way and a bad way to apply moisturizers or cleansing products. Ask the salesperson to demonstrate the best way to apply them.

LET'S GO HAVE A GOOD TIME

If you experience anxiety in crowded clubs or bars, try these:

Easiest: Go to a local sports bar on a weeknight and have dinner.

Moderate: Go to a local sports bar during happy hour on a Thursday or Friday evening. Strike up a conversation.

Difficult: Go to a popular dance club on a weekend and strike up a conversation with the bartender and people you find attractive.

LET'S GO TO THE CITY

If being in a very active and stimulating environment with a lot of people makes you anxious, go to your nearest crowded city and try these:

Easiest: Walk around a quieter neighborhood. Try to stop for a cup of coffee in a neighborhood café.

Moderate: Walk around the business district during lunch time. Try to eat at a sandwich shop.

Difficult: Spend time in a train, bus, or subway station during the evening rush hour.

Reducing Reassurance Seeking: Common Pitfalls

Perhaps you feel that you need others to reassure you that you're attractive, that you look good in the photo, that your stomach isn't sticking out, that your arms are normal, that your complexion isn't full of pimples, that your lips aren't too small or too big, that your teeth are white and not misshapen, that your penis is normal size and not crooked, that your hair looks good, that your breasts don't sag, that your nose isn't pointed or drooping, that your face and body isn't full of hair, and so on. We can go on and on about what you might find disgusting about yourself and how you need others to tell you that you are "aces" in their book. Well, what happens after they give you that reassurance? Several things may occur: you may actually feel relieved and good for a while, you may discount their reassurance, you may think they're lying to you, or you may think they're in no position to evaluate your appearance so you seek other people for reassurance. Reassurance seeking may relieve distress for a little while, but the thoughts keep coming back. It's just like mirror checking: even when it makes you feel good, the bad feelings don't go away. Do you discount reassurance or compliments? Maybe you tell yourself *They love me, so of course they think I'm attractive* or *They don't want me to feel bad, so they say what they think I want to hear.* No matter what, you'll most likely not feel good for long with any assurance you get. When you have a need to ask someone about your appearance, think back to the last time you asked. What happened? Were you satisfied and, if so, for how long? Did it help you in the long run? Probably not, and in fact it probably perpetuated the desire to seek reassurance. That is how rituals or compulsions work. The more you give in, the more they haunt you. Remember these words: "response prevention"—and prevent yourself from asking next time. Do something else instead: take a walk, take a bath or shower, exercise, get on the computer, or do an exposure exercise.

Dealing with Technology

Technology makes life harder for individuals with BDD because everyone uses their phones to take pictures, videotape, and even to videochat and access social networking websites. No matter where you turn, you're faced with an opportunity to compare yourself to someone else. What can you do to avoid falling into that pit? Don't avoid using any of these technologies because of fear. Fear should never guide your behaviors. Of course it's natural for all of us to want to avoid those things that make us fearful, sad, disgusted, or ashamed, but to conquer negative feelings, we need to face them.

Let's start with what you avoid using these days and make a list of what you want to tackle first. Can you take a picture of yourself with your phone and use it as your wallpaper? Can you have a family member videotape you reading a passage out of book, reciting poetry, telling a joke, or talking about something and then watch it? Or, as we suggested earlier, get on a social networking website and post a picture, even if it initially needs to be a group picture or one in which your image isn't very clear. Start videochatting with the people you're most comfortable with and then, over time, graduate to those whose judgment you fear. Who will be the first person you videochat with? Who will be the second, third, and so forth? Are you getting the idea? Use all the technology available to you. Start today!

Skin Picking

Now we'd like to discuss a behavior that challenges many people who suffer from BDD: skin picking. In this section, you'll learn some strategies to decrease skin picking. As you may remember from chapter 1, people who are concerned with acne and other skin imperfections often engage in skin picking as a way to improve their appearance. Unfortunately, most people who skin pick quickly realize they're stuck in a negative cycle that makes their skin look worse. The damage from picking typically leads to skin irritation, scars, and blemishes. Many of the clients we've treated describe experiencing a temporary sense of accomplishment from picking. As one twenty-seven-year-old BDD sufferer stated, "When I pick, I feel like I'm actually doing something productive to improve my skin. It's only later when I actually look at the damage that I realize how much worse I've made it."

Picking can consist of digging, scratching, squeezing, or using tools, such as tweezers, to remove acne, bumps, whiteheads, or other impurities. Although the initial motivation is to improve one's appearance, the behavior can take on a life of its own. It can begin to serve other functions, such as stress reduction, relief from boredom, or a way to relax, or it can simply become a habit. Interestingly, many people with BDD note that sensory experiences can trigger their picking. They may "feel" skin tightening, itching, or some kind of discomfort. This leads to touching their skin, which can trigger the skin picking.

Techniques for Reducing Picking

In the 1970s, researchers Nathan Azrin and Robert Nunn published articles introducing a treatment for habits and tics called habit reversal training (HRT). In the following sections, we'll incorporate HRT techniques— awareness and competing response training—with cognitive therapy and coping strategies to help you reduce your picking.

AWARENESS TRAINING

The first step in HRT is to build awareness of the behavior. *Awareness training* brings more attention to and knowledge about the behavior. If you don't know you're doing something, you can't change it. Try the following two exercises to build more awareness of your picking.

EXERCISE: Where, When, How, and Why Do You Pick?

Use the chart below to keep track of your skin picking for the next week. You can use the log below by making photocopies or transcribing it into your notebook.

SKIN PICKING CHART

Where were you?	What time of day?	What were you doing?	How did you pick?	Why did you pick? What triggered your picking?	Note any thoughts that went through your mind as you picked.	Note your emotions at the time.	What are the consequences to your picking? How did you feel after? How does your skin look afterward?

When you fill in the first column—*Where were you?*—you might say, for example, "at the bathroom mirror," "in the car," "sitting on couch." In the fourth column—*How did you pick?*—indicate whether you picked with your fingers, tweezers, or something else. In the fifth column—*Why did you pick? What triggered your picking?*—you might answer, for example, "boredom," "stress," "habit," "itchy feeling on my cheek," "I noticed a red bump and had to remove it," "feeling for bumps," "looking in mirror," and so on. In the column *Note your emotions at the time*, indicate if you were anxious, restless, frustrated, bored, or angry, or if you felt some other emotion.

After a week, look back at the chart carefully. Is there a pattern to your picking behavior? What are your most vulnerable times of day and situations? Do you mostly pick out of habit or due to BDD thoughts? These are extremely important observations.

Here's another exercise to develop awareness of your skin picking. In this exercise, you'll become very aware of every detail of a picking episode.

EXERCISE: Describe the Picking

The next time you pick, pay close attention to where you are, what triggers your urge to pick, and how you go about picking. Describe this episode to an imaginary audience. Pretend that your audience is blind. Tell your audience which hand you used and what you felt on your skin. Did you feel around until you found a particular bump? Did you start by rubbing the bump and then squeezing it out?

Both these exercises should help you become an expert on your picking. Now use the next exercise to summarize what you've learned about your picking.

EXERCISE: What Did You Learn about Your Picking?

Use your skin picking chart to answer these questions. This should help you be more aware of what situations, emotions, thoughts, and activities typically trigger your picking.

- List the most common places you pick (car, couch, in bed).

- List the most common activities that trigger your picking (driving, being online, watching TV, feeling for bumps).

- List the thoughts that trigger your picking.

- List all the emotions that trigger your picking.

- How often did you feel better after picking? How often did you feel worse?

You can now use strategies to decrease your picking. Most of the treatment strategies for picking are based on first recognizing what brought on your urge to pick and then finding an appropriate replacement or solution.

Coping and Problem Solving

Hopefully through awareness training you've noticed some patterns in your picking and have started to form some ideas to help reduce it. Here are some strategies to decrease your picking. We've categorized them by thoughts, emotions, and behaviors.

PICKING TRIGGERED BY BDD THOUGHTS

If your picking is typically due to BDD thoughts, then go back to your cognitive therapy skills and challenge your thoughts.

Here are some common thoughts we've heard from our clients who skin pick:

- *I will just pick this one pimple and then leave my skin alone.*

- *I have to get rid of this one pimple or it will look worse.*

- *I need perfectly smooth skin.*

- *Picking sometimes does work to get rid of my pimples.*

Can you find ways to challenge and replace these thoughts with more rational observations? How often have you bargained with yourself to just pick once and stop? How often has that worked? Does your skin really look better if you get rid of one pimple?

PICKING TRIGGERED BY EMOTIONS

If your picking has taken other roles as a way to cope with emotions, we encourage you to first use your cognitive therapy skills. Although picking is usually triggered by negative emotions, such as boredom, stress, anger, irritability, nervousness, restlessness, and sadness, many of our clients have picked when excited or anticipating a positive situation. Notice what triggers your negative emotions. What are you doing and thinking? Perhaps your thoughts are extreme and unhealthy given the situation. Is there another, less extreme way to view the situation? Return to the cognitive therapy chapter and use the recommended techniques.

There are many other strategies for coping with negative emotions. Here are a few: Do you notice that you're more vulnerable to negative emotions when you are tired or hungry? Meeting your body's daily needs by getting plenty of rest, eating well-balanced meals, and exercising will reduce your tendency to experience extreme negative emotions. Do you experience more negative emotions when you rush around because you've avoided completing some necessary chores or have overbooked yourself? Then practicing better time management may help reduce your overall stress. Maybe you need to incorporate more relaxation time into your life by engaging in activities you enjoy. Habit reversal training recommends relaxation and breathing strategies as an effective strategy. Enrolling in a yoga or meditation class can be very helpful. Identifying triggers for negative emotions and finding ways to meet your emotional needs can help reduce your urges to pick.

PICKING TRIGGERED BY SITUATIONS OR ACTIVITIES (HABIT-BASED PICKING)

It's quite common for skin picking to become a habit for people with BDD. If your picking has become associated with certain times of day, certain activities, and certain situations, you're not alone. Do you find yourself picking at the end of the day while watching TV? Do you pick while driving even if you're not necessarily focused on a particular pimple?

If your picking is habit based, the second component of habit reversal training—competing response training—may be useful to you. *Competing response training* is a way to build substitute behaviors to do instead of picking. In essence, find creative ways to keep your hands occupied and away from your skin. Here are some ideas: playing with Silly Putty, popping the bubbles in plastic packaging, knitting, playing video games, picking at the fuzzy parts of an old sweater, giving yourself a manicure, or fiddling with beaded jewelry.

Another way to reduce picking due to habit is to make it hard to pick. This includes strategies like putting bandage strips on your fingers, using a sticky moisturizer on your hands, cutting your nails very short, or wearing cotton gloves.

KEY TO EFFECTIVE STRATEGIES: BE PREPARED

The key to making these strategies as effective as possible is to be prepared. Look back at your awareness exercises and note the situations and times of day you tend to pick. Keep your competing response strategies easily accessible in your situations. Put a basket of toys to fiddle with on your coffee table. Place some bandage strips and gloves in the basket. It's much easier to use strategies *before* you've started picking. Most people tell us how hard it is to stop once they've started to pick.

Skin picking is a challenging habit for many people, whether with or without BDD. Don't be discouraged if you don't see improvement right away. Review these strategies regularly and adjust as needed—add new ones and throw out the ones that don't work. Replace your substitute behaviors often so you don't get bored with the ones you have. We're confident that these techniques can help you gain control.

It's never easy to face your fears directly. Exposure and response prevention is a tough treatment. But remember, years of research have proven that it works. The treatment doesn't have to be done in a week. It can take people many months to tackle their whole hierarchy. Don't worry—you'll start feeling better as you do the exposure exercises. Remember to set realistic goals and reward yourself for small accomplishments. Once you've mastered your hierarchy, it's beneficial to repeat the exercises regularly to maintain the progress.

7

Attentional Training and Imagery Rescripting

Do you have difficulty paying attention to what's going on around you? Do you feel you live in your head? In the previous chapters, you learned how to challenge your thinking and then how to behave differently. Now we'll make some suggestions on how to use attentional training and imagery rescripting to help you get out of your head and pay attention to the world around you.

If you're like other people with BDD, you focus your attention on your own thoughts, negative mental images, and feelings. In other words, you focus on yourself. You observe yourself as if you were someone else observing you, and you may be even more focused on what you're doing, feeling, imagining, and thinking when you're in social situations. In this chapter, you'll learn how to change and balance your focus.

Attentional Training: Learning to Shift Your Focus Off of Yourself

It's important to pay attention to your environment and to get out of your mind in order to participate in life. We call this "attentional training." *Attentional training* (Wells 2000) involves refocusing of attention as well as task concentration skills. *Refocusing of attention* means learning to go outside of yourself and become aware of sounds, colors, and sights in your environment. In short, you pay attention to the outside world and not what you're thinking and feeling. In *task concentration*, you pay attention to what's being said or discussed; in other words, you refocus from your inner thoughts to words spoken by others. You concentrate on others, not on yourself.

Refocusing Your Attention

Refocusing your attention, or what therapists sometimes call *attentional refocusing*, changes the focus of your attention from yourself (an "internal" focus) to the world around you (an "external" focus). The goal of attentional refocusing is to move away from this pattern of self-focused attention and instead to focus more on your external environment. When you're anxious, being able to shift your attention outward allows you to modify your negative beliefs about yourself. For example, if you're sitting in a class or a meeting and you're focusing on your skin or hair and thinking about how others are viewing you, you'll need to refocus your attention on what is being taught or talked about in the meeting. In time, you may realize that no one is really concerned about your looks. If you find yourself comparing your disliked body part with that body part in someone else, you'll find it helpful to focus instead on the sounds, smells, colors, or other aspects of your immediate environment.

To shift your attention from an internal focus to an external one, you first need to be aware of what you're focusing on. The exercises below will help you see where you place your focus.

EXERCISE: Monitoring the Focus of Your Attention

Choose three time periods when you're engaged in different activities, such as watching TV, talking to someone, or exercising. During those times, observe how self-focused you are, how preoccupied you are with your body part of concern, and what level of distress you experience. Rate your experience using a scale of 0 to 10 (0 = totally self-focused; 10 = totally externally focused). Complete self-focused attention is when you only pay attention to your own thoughts, feelings, and mental images of yourself. A complete external focus is when you focus only on the outside world. When your focus is balanced (5 on the scale), your attention is equally divided between yourself and your environment. Record your numbers in the chart below or transcribe the chart into your notebook.

Date	Situation	How Self-Focused I Was (0–10)	Degree of Preoccupation with Body Part(s) of Concern (0–10)	Level of Distress (0–10)

Each day review your chart above and see if you can identify particular situations where you are excessively self-focused. Is it when you're anxious or somehow feel threatened, such as when you're in the presence of someone you compare yourself to? Becoming aware of when you're most self-focused is the first step toward learning how to shift from an internal focus to an external focus.

As you work toward becoming more aware, it's important not to confuse awareness with hypervilance. *Hypervigilance* is a heightened state of alertness or awareness and usually involves carefully watching your environment for signs of danger. It's important to learn how not to be hypervilant because when you're overly aware of how others look at you, you may perceive a threat where there is none. Do you find yourself scanning for threats in your environment? As you scan, do you find yourself getting more preoccupied and more upset about your appearance? You may notice that you're comparing your features to those of other people. You may, for example, misinterpret someone's glances or comments as a negative evaluation of your appearance even though, in reality, that person didn't even notice you. In this next exercise, let's look at how hypervigilant you are to cues in your environment.

EXERCISE: Monitoring Your Hypervigilance

Once a day for fifteen minutes over the next several weeks, monitor your hypervigilance using the list below. Check off what causes you to be hypervigilant.

I am hypervigilant to:

_____ Compliments

_____ Criticism

_____ People laughing

_____ People looking at me

_____ People who are more attractive

_____ To nature

_____ To texture, sound, colors in my environment

_____ To music

_____ Other _____

Now that you're more aware of situations in which you're self-focused and hypervigilant, you need next to learn how to decrease your self-focus and increase your external focus. Your goal is to shift this pattern of narrowly focused attention to a more holistic, broader approach. This will help you spend less time on BDD thoughts and feelings.

Decreasing Self-Focus

It's important to decrease your self-focus in order not to think negatively about your appearance. By focusing your attention on your environment and on conversations with others, you'll take the focus off of yourself.

Ironically, however, one of the ways to decrease your self-focus is to first increase it, as you will do in the first exercise below. Ask a friend or family member to assist you by being your partner in the following two exercises. For these exercises, you'll also need a quiet space, two chairs, and a full-length mirror. Do these exercises once a day for fifteen minutes.

EXERCISE: Self-Focus and Discussing a Neutral Topic

Bring your partner into a quiet room with you. As we mentioned above, you'll first increase your self-focus so that you can train yourself to decrease it. To increase your self-focus, do one of the following: ask your partner to stare at you, look at yourself in the mirror, or ruminate about your particular body part of concern. Think about the way you feel. Rate how self-focused, preoccupied, and distressed you are and put the numbers in the chart below. Keep your self-focus high.

Date	Situation	How Self-Focused I Was (0–10)	Degree of Preoccupation with Body Part(s) of Concern (0–10)	Level of Distress (0–10)

Now sit with your back turned to your partner. Talk to your partner about a very neutral subject, such as a trip, a movie you saw, a book you read, or a hobby you have. When you finish, once again rate how self-focused, preoccupied, and distressed you are. Write the numbers on the chart.

Next, repeat this exercise facing your partner. Again, when you've finished talking, rate how self-focused, preoccupied, and distressed you are. Write the numbers on the chart.

EXERCISE: Self-Focus and Discussing a Threatening Topic

Repeat the exercise above, but this time talk about a threatening topic, such as people whose appearance you admire or how appearance gets you all the things that are valuable. Rate again how self-focused, preoccupied, and distressed you are, and then write the numbers on the chart.

How did you pay attention to yourself in each of the exercises above? Was there a difference between your focus in the first exercise and in the second one? How did your focus differ?

The next step in refocusing your attention is to decrease your attention on yourself and increase your attention to what's going on around you—that is, to shift your attention from an internal to an external focus.

SHIFTING ATTENTION FROM INTERNAL TO EXTERNAL FOCUS

When you shift from an internal to an external focus, you're training yourself to pay attention to what's happening *around* you rather than what's happening *inside* you. To do this, pay attention to all aspects of your environment: become more aware of the sounds, textures, and sights around you. You can do this when you're alone or with other people; in public or social situations, be more attentive to what people say and do.

If you find it difficult to switch your attention from internal to external focus, you may find it helpful to explore your reasons for being self-focused—that is, why you feel you want or need to be self-focused. For example, you might use a picture of yourself as a portable "internal mirror" that can be easily carried around. What's the reason for this? You do it to check your appearance internally so you can know exactly what you look like at all times (especially when there's no external mirror available). The next exercise will help you explore the reasons for your self-focus.

EXERCISE: Exploring the Reasons for Your Self-Focus

The questions below will help you explore your reasons for focusing on yourself—on your thoughts, feelings, and mental images. Take your time and write your answers in your notebook.

- What are my reasons for being self-focused?

    I feel that being self-focused will help me with

    1. _____

2. _____

3. _____

- Do these reasons help me accomplish my goals and live by my values?

- Do I think other people should be self-focused? Why?

- Is it possible that others may see me differently than I see myself? What influences my impression of myself over time?

- Do I have doubts about focusing my attention externally? What are those doubts?

- Are there ways in which being self-focused isn't helpful for me?

Your answers to these questions may help you understand why you find it difficult to focus externally. For example, you may have reservations about changing your focus because you think that if you're not self-focused, you'll become careless about your appearance. You may think *I need to be self-focused so I can look the best I can.* Or you may have some obstacles that prevent you from changing your focus, such as very important events coming up for which you need to make sure you look your best. Once you identify your obstacles to changing your focus, you can challenge your thoughts, as we discussed in chapter 5.

UNDERSTANDING HOW AND WHY YOU SELF-FOCUS

Sometimes it can be very challenging to switch attention—to go from internal to external focus. When this occurs, it's helpful to discover the "functional" purpose for your self-focused attention—that is, how and why you self-focus. This can help you recognize patterns and even triggers of self-focused attention. The exercise below asks you some questions. Your responses can help you identify some explanations for your self-focused attention.

EXERCISE: Why and How Do You Self-Focus?

Take some time to reflect on the questions below. Write your answers in your notebook.

- **What happened?** Please describe a recent situation in which you were self-focused.

- **What was your behavior?** Please describe what you were doing to be excessively self-focused.

- **What did you hope to do?** Before you started being self-focused, what did you want to accomplish?

- **What happened as an immediate result?** Was there a positive outcome for being self-focused? Did you feel you were doing something to prevent something bad from happening? For example, were you trying to make sure you were looking good by comparing yourself to someone else and wishing you would look like that person?

- **What was the ultimate result?** What effect did being self-focused have? Did it make you more preoccupied with your appearance? Did it make you more anxious? What effect did being self-focused have on your friends and family?

- **What else could have you done?** Would being externally focused be more consistent with your values and goals?

Now see if you can identify a pattern in your answers to these questions. You may notice, for example, that self-focusing keeps your anxiety and distress level down, helps you feel in control, or makes you believe that you can change the way you look if you concentrate on it enough. Remember Ana, who was preoccupied with her skin? Her reason for being self-focused was that she believed if she focused on the external world, she wouldn't be able to come up with ways to improve her skin.

Shifting your attention from internal to external focus and under-standing your reasons for self-focusing aren't the only way to decrease your self-focus. Let's take a look now at a few other helpful strategies.

OTHER STRATEGIES TO DECREASE SELF-FOCUS

Now let's look at some other strategies to decrease self-focus. These will help you shift your attention away from yourself and help you to see the world around you—that is, help you move from an internal focus to an external focus.

Use detached mindfulness. You've probably tried avoiding or suppressing intrusive thoughts and images. You probably weren't very successful, not because of who you are but because most of us can't will away a thought. However, we can learn to use detached mindfulness, a fancy term that means you recognize the thought and then just observe it. You separate the thought from yourself by saying, "I have the thought that my skin is full of bumps," "I have the thought that my nose is big," or "I have a thought that says my hair is too curly." Learning detached mindfulness can help you in the process of defusion, which means not becoming obsessed with a thought—that is, letting go of a thought after recognizing it.

A useful analogy for detached mindfulness is that of traffic on the road: Imagine your thoughts and feelings are cars passing on the road. When you're consumed with intrusive thoughts and images, you focus on particular "cars" that tell you that you're unattractive or just not good enough. You may react by trying to stop the car or flag it down, or you may even attempt to get in the driver's seat and park the car. However, no matter what you do, more cars keep coming. Detached mindfulness means acknowledging the cars and the traffic, but, instead of reacting to them, you just notice them and continue walking along the street. You focus your attention on other parts of your environment, such as the friend who's walking beside you. The thoughts have no more meaning than the cars passing by. The thoughts are just thoughts; they're like traffic noise in the background. Just notice the thoughts and feelings and acknowledge their presence—and then let them go.

Switch your focus of attention. Attentional training (ATT) helps you increase your ability to switch your attention from yourself to the world around you. It works by having you focus your attention outward onto sounds. The point of ATT is not to distract yourself when you're distressed or ruminating, but rather to teach you different ways to use and focus your attention. Try the exercise below to practice switching your focus of attention.

EXERCISE: Listening to the Sounds around You

In this exercise, you'll focus on sounds in different ways—one at a time, switching your attention among the sounds, and then all at the same time. The sounds might be, for example, a running faucet, the TV on in the next room, or the traffic outside. Try to identify eight sounds and then number them. For example, sound 1 may be the running faucet, sound 2 may be the TV in the next room, and so on. Try to pick sounds that are continuous (that is, not intermittent or occasional), and be sure that one sound doesn't overpower the other.

Find a comfortable place to sit and relax. Try your best to keep your eyes open throughout this exercise. It may help to focus on one spot on the wall. If thoughts, feelings, or mental images distract you during the exercise, that's okay. Just notice the distractions and then refocus your attention on the sounds. The goal is to practice focusing your attention in a specific way.

This exercise has three phases. Complete each phase before going on to the next one. Before you begin the first phase, identify eight sounds that you hear and then number them. When you've done that, move on to phase 1.

Phase 1

Pay close attention to sound 1 only. Ignore all other sounds. Now switch focus to sound 2. Again, ignore all other sounds except sound 2. If your attention strays, do your best to refocus. Go through all the sounds. This will take up to eight minutes, with one minute per sound.

Phase 2

In phase 1, you focused on the sounds one by one. In this phase, shift your attention rapidly from one sound to another in a random order. For example, you could pass from sound 6 to sound 4 to sound 3 to sound 5 to sound 1, and so on. As before, focus all your attention on one sound before switching your attention to a different sound. This phase will take about five minutes.

Phase 3

Now expand all your attention—make it as broad as possible—and try to absorb all the sounds simultaneously. Mentally count all the sounds you can hear at the same time. This phase will take about two minutes.

Practice this exercise at least once a day (preferably twice) for about fifteen minutes. If possible, find new sounds to use each time you practice. As time goes by, add more sounds and incorporate sounds from different locations.

Note: By recording sounds on a CD or MP3 player, you receive the benefit of introducing sounds that are more interesting and varied. However, you may lose the spatial location—that is, the ability to focus your attention to different locations—if it's not recorded and played back with surround sound. Whether the sounds are recorded or live, they should be fairly continuous (that is, not intermittent) and should change over time to prevent repetition. It's important to keep a diary of your practice (see "Record of Attention Training" below). In addition to the date and time of your practice, how many sounds you used, and the degree of self-focused attention (using the scale 0 to 10), also note how long you practiced and whether you experienced any difficulties as you practiced. As we mentioned before, the goal is not to suppress thoughts or images, but to practice focusing attention on other things—in this case, sounds. If internal events, such as thoughts or sensations, do intrude, try not to react but to refocus your attention to the external world.

RECORD OF ATTENTION TRAINING

Rate your level of self-focus (0 = entirely self-focused; 10 = entirely externally focused). A 5 indicates that your attention is divided equally between being self-focused and externally focused.

Date/ Time	How self-focused I have been generally today (0–10)	How long I practiced	Number of sounds I used	Any other comments

Switch your focus of attention—variations. There are other attentional strategies that encourage increasing flexibility by switching attention in non-anxiety-provoking situations. First, focus on your environment rather than yourself in nonsocial situations. Then do the same in social situations. As you practice, focus on the different sounds, colors, objects, textures, smells, and events in your environment. Then switch from one thing to another—for instance, from the sounds of birds in the park to the color of the flowers to the texture of the grass, and so on.

EXERCISE: Increasing Flexibility of Attention

Learning to switch the focus of your attention from one thing to another in your environment teaches you flexibility. This is important because as you focus on external things, self-focused attention should decrease.

Becoming Aware of Different Sounds and Sights

Practice indoors by trying one of the following activities.

- Listen to music on the computer or on the radio: pay attention to the different instruments that are playing (guitar, keyboard, drums, bass, saxophone, and so on).

- Sit quietly and pay attention to the sounds in the room and sounds you can hear outside.

- Pay attention to objects, colors, textures, and smells in the room.

Practice outdoor by trying one of the following activities.

- Go for a walk in the park: pay attention to the sounds in your environment, both the sounds in close proximity and the sounds in the distance.

- Pay attention to the objects in the environment around you: buildings, plants, trees, traffic, and people. What colors, textures, and shapes do you see? What types of people do you see?

Switching Your Attention between the Different Sounds and Sights

The next step is to switch your attention among the different sounds and sights in your environment.

1. Choose three sounds.

2. Focus on one of the sounds, noticing as much as possible about the sound—its quality, strength, volume, pitch, and so on.

3. If your attention shifts to something else, bring it back to the first sound.

4. After following the first sound for about a minute, shift attention to another sound and become absorbed in that sound.

5. Repeat this for a third sound.

6. Move on to colors, objects, and textures. As you did with the sounds, focus on each one for about a minute, noticing as much as possible about it, and then move on to the next one.

Pulling It All Together

Once you've focused on a number of different sounds and sights, try to become aware of all of them at once.

1. Allow all of the sights and sounds to fill your attention.

2. Allow yourself to become lost in the outside world.

3. If your attention shifts back toward yourself, just acknowledge the shift and refocus your attention on the outside world.

Once you learn to be more flexible and shift your attention from one sound to another, and from sounds to textures to colors, and so on, you'll get a feeling for living in the outside world as opposed to living in your head. You'll pay more attention to what's going on around you.

The next step is to learn how to direct your attention in conversations. This is usually difficult for people with BDD. You're probably so focused on your internal world that you find it difficult to focus on what's being discussed. Task concentration training will help you with this.

Task Concentration Training

Similar to attentional refocusing, *task concentration training* (TCT) is an attention-training procedure aimed at helping you direct your attention away from the self and toward the task and environment. Tasks might include listening and/or talking to others in different situations, reading a book, watching a movie, or doing some other activity. For example, you may be involved in a classroom discussion with a very attractive classmate sitting next to you or you may be discussing with a very good friend a trip to the zoo. Certainly the first activity or task may be more anxiety producing or distressful than the latter. Task concentration training has been used in social phobia (Bögels 2006), fear of blushing (Mulkens, Bögels, and De Jong 1999; Mulkens et al. 2001), and BDD (Mulkens 2007).

Task concentration training consists of three phases:

1. Gaining insight into the role of attention and the effects of heightened self-focused attention

2. Focusing attention outward in nonthreatening situations

3. Focusing attention outward in threatening situations

Phase 1: Gaining Insight through Task Concentration Training

Tracking attentional focus allows you to monitor the way information is processed and provides insight into the way your attention is divided in situations that trigger negative self-evaluation and anxiety. The first step in gaining insight is to monitor the degree of your attention in different contexts. Record these on the chart below or create a table in your notebook:

- Date and time

- Situation

- The percentage of concentration that you directed at that moment toward yourself, the task, and your environment. These ratings must add up to 100 percent. (For example, regarding a conversation with a friend, you may report 70 percent of your attention was on yourself, 20 percent was on the conversation, and 10 percent was on your environment; an individual without BDD would most likely report the opposite: 70 percent on the conversation, 20 percent on the self, and 10 percent on the environment.)

- The degree of preoccupation, using a scale of X to 10 (X = entirely self-focused; Y = equally divided between internal and external focus; 10 = entirely externally focused), and degree of distress, using a scale of X to 10 (X = no distress; Y = moderate distress; 10 = extreme distress).

TASK CONCENTRATION TRAINING

Date/Time	Situation	Attention to Self (0–100%)	Attention to Task (0–100%)	Attention to Environment (0–100%)	Preoccupation (0–10)	Distress (0–10)

Below are some task concentration exercises that you can do with a friend or a family member. For these exercises, you'll need a quiet space, two chairs, and a full-length mirror. The exercises will help you become a better listener. They'll help you concentrate on what someone is talking about or focus on the topic at hand rather than on your appearance and negative feelings. Use the chart above to record the results of each exercise.

EXERCISE: Gaining Insight through Listening #1

Sit with your back toward your partner so that you have no eye contact. Have your partner tell you a neutral story for two minutes. For example, your partner can tell you a story about a play he saw, a restaurant he went to, or a trip he took. Try to concentrate on the story; try to recall the whole story. When the story is over, try to summarize it. Estimate the percentage of attention that you directed toward yourself, toward the task (the story), and toward your environment. Also, estimate the percentage of the story that you were able to summarize and then have your partner do the same. You may feel that this task isn't very difficult for you.

EXERCISE: Gaining Insight through Listening #2

For this exercise, sit facing your partner so that you make eye contact. Have your partner tell you another two-minute story. As in the first listening exercise, try to concentrate on the story and summarize it afterward. Estimate the percentage of attention you directed toward self, task, and environment, and then both you and your partner estimate the percentage of the story you were able to summarize. You may notice that you became more self-focused because of the eye contact and as a result remembered less of the story than in the first exercise.

EXERCISE: Gaining Insight through Listening #3

Have your partner tell you another two-minute story. This time distract yourself from listening by thinking about something that evokes fear of negative evaluation, such as *My partner is thinking that my hair is really gross.* Or, instead of thinking about something, you may touch the body part of concern or look at yourself in the mirror. (It's good to have the mirror next to the person who's telling the story.) Then try to refocus your attention on the story and summarize it afterward. As in the previous listening exercises, estimate the percentage of attention you directed toward yourself, the task, and your environment, and then both you and your partner estimate the percentage of the story you were able to summarize. Typically, self-focused attention increases when you think about your problem. As a result, you may notice gaps in your summarization of the story, especially at the moments where you thought about someone evaluating you negatively, when you were touching your body part(s) of concern, or when you looked in the mirror.

EXERCISE: Gaining Insight through Listening #4

For this exercise, have your partner tell you another two-minute story, one that causes you to have negative thoughts about yourself—for example, meeting somebody who has a large nose, if this is your main body part of concern. (The idea here is for your partner to make up a story about someone having a concern similar to yours.) When your partner finishes the story, summarize it. As in the previous listening exercises, estimate the percentage of attention you directed toward yourself, the task, and your environment, and then both you and your partner estimate the percentage of the story you were able to summarize.

Repeat all four exercises until you focus at least 51 percent of your attention on the task. Achieving this may take a long time, sometimes even months, so don't get discouraged.

Due to the more complex elements in exercises #3 and #4, most people at first become more self-focused, but, after some practice, they're able to refocus on the task. Also, practicing the more complex exercises helps you increase your resistance to distraction.

EXERCISE: Gaining Insight through Speaking

The speaking exercises are practiced in the same way as the listening exercises above. You will tell your partner a two-minute story, while concentrating on the task (speaking and observing whether your partner listens and understands the story you're telling). The speaking exercises also involve all four steps above. Repeat all four exercises with you doing the talking. Record the results on the chart above. You can use the log above by making photocopies or transcribing it into you notebook.

Phase 2: Using Task Concentration Training in Nonthreatening Situations

Now that you've practiced concentrating on others talking while you listen (and vice versa), it's time to focus on other types of activities. This is important because your focus can turn to yourself not only when others are talking but also when you're engaged in other activities, such as listening to music, watching a show, and so on. The following exercises will help you focus on various tasks or activities rather than on yourself.

EXERCISE: Dealing with Nonthreatening Situations

Practice moving from internal to external focus every day in nonthreatening situations. This will help your ability to focus away from your BDD.

First, walk outside and pay attention to all aspects of your environment. What do you see? Smell? Hear? Feel?

Second, pay attention—one at a time—to your own body sensations (your heart beating, your breathing, how warm or cold you are, how often you're blinking, and so on).

Third, listen to instrumental music. Begin by deliberately focusing on one instrument. Next, switch your focus to another instrument. Try to focus on at least five different instruments. Finally, integrate and listen to all the instruments at once—that is, listen to the piece of music as a whole.

When you switch your focus from one instrument to another, you're practicing *flexible attention*. When you integrate all aspects by listening to the piece of music as a whole, you're practicing *integrated attention*. You've become focused on the activity or task instead of your thoughts or feelings.

Phase 3: Using Task Concentration Training in Threatening Situations

Task concentration training can help you cope in threatening situations by having you focus on the activity or task instead of your thoughts or feelings. TCT in threatening situations involves these aspects:

- Monitor your attention—that is, what you're focusing on.

- Determine what the task at hand is.

- Determine whether your attention keeps changing.

- Practice focusing on the task.

- Evaluate the percentage of your focus on the task versus on yourself.

- Increase task focus by paying attention to what you see, hear, do, and so on.

- Practice until you focus on the task more than 51 percent of the time.

Don't become discouraged if you're not able to do this all the first time you try it. This may take a long time to achieve, sometimes even weeks or months.

EXERCISE: Dealing with Threatening Situations

Make a list of ten situations where you focus on yourself and where you think negatively of yourself. Rate these situations from 1 (least self-focused) to 10 (highly self-focused).

By rating these situations, you've created a hierarchy based on your self-focus. In chapter 6, you created a hierarchy based on degree of discomfort. Compare that hierarchy to this one. Is there some overlap? Are they the same?

Now, to deal with these threatening situations, practice paying attention to the task at hand rather than focusing on yourself. Situations can be practiced using role-plays with a partner.

Here's an example of how this might work. If you avoid speaking to a cosmetics salesperson because you don't want her to notice your skin, you can role-play with a partner going to a store and asking to be shown makeup or hair products. In your role-play, ask for the product, paying attention to what you're saying and how your partner responds. Also, pay attention to sounds, textures, lighting, and colors in your environment. When you finish the role-play, estimate how much of the conversation about the product you recall.

Or role-play that you're at an appliance store inquiring about toaster ovens. As you speak, you think the salesperson is noticing your hairline. Instead of focusing on that, pay attention to your environment—the various products, the lighting, the number of people, the various types of toasters, how they differ, what they cost, and so on. At the end of the role-play, see how much of the conversation you remember. In addition to doing a role-play with a partner, try doing this in a real appliance department.

Make sure you incorporate decreasing self-focus and increasing attention to tasks and your external environment in all situations every day. As you practice, you'll notice that it gets easier.

You've worked hard in the first part of this chapter! You've learned to focus your attention away from yourself. You've also learned to listen better to others whether they're talking about neutral topics or topics that upset you. In addition, you've learned to become a better speaker and to engage in activities without resorting to old habits of thinking about your body. Hopefully, all of the exercises above have helped you become more flexible and more involved in your environment.

Next, we'll look at how you view yourself in your mind. Our body image is based on a mental representation of what we *think* we look like, not necessarily how we actually look. This is true for all of us. Sometimes it's important to change the mental image we have of ourselves. In the next section, we'll see how imagery rescripting can help you view yourself differently.

Imagery Rescripting: Changing Your Images of Yourself

We all have mental images of our memories and experiences as well as images of our self and our body. If you think of the particular body part that you dislike, you may evoke all kinds of mental images, and those mental images trigger negative self-evaluations (for example, feelings of ugliness) and lead to compulsive responses (such as ruminations and safety-seeking behaviors). When Katie, for example, thinks about her large nose (mental image), she thinks she's unattractive and will never get a date (negative self-evaluation), which then leads her to mirror check (compulsive response). Our images of ourselves—and how we think and feel about them—are powerful. So if we have negative images, what can we do about them? How can imagery rescripting help?

Do you have mental images of negative experiences, such as being teased or bullied at school, being self-conscious about your appearance during puberty, having acne, or being physically or sexually abused? In addition to having mental images of those negative experiences, you may also have bodily sensations connected with them. That's because imagery is multisensory. For example, maybe you were teased for having acne as a teenager. Your mental image may include not only how you looked, but also the bodily sensations of how you felt at the time, including feelings of shame, self-consciousness, and disgust.

Imagery rescripting (Artnz and Weertman 1999; Smucker and Dancu 1999) refers to changing your mental images, whether those images reflect the way you view your body in your mind or the way you view and interpret a negative event that happened in the past. Imagery rescripting has been found by researchers to be effective with trauma-based experiences (such as child abuse, rape, and war atrocities), aversive experiences (such as being bullied or teased), and experiences associated with the onset of an image in the mind (for example, looking in the mirror and seeing yourself as ugly). Imagery rescripting can help you change the way you view yourself in your mind—that is, the mental image you have about the way you look.

The goals of imagery rescripting in BDD are to

- develop a different relationship with the intrusive image;

- question the accuracy and validity of the meaning of the image; and

- develop a compassionate and caring approach to yourself.

Imagery rescripting consists of three stages:

1. Assessing your images

2. Reliving your experience

3. Repeating and rescripting your memory from an adult perspective

The stages are highlighted below and include helpful exercises. The exercises walk you through each of the stages as you seek to rescript painful images in your own life. They involve much self-reflection. You may choose to reflect by writing in your notebook, or, if you prefer, you may go through these stages with a friend or family member in whom you feel comfortable confiding.

Assessing Your Images

As we mentioned above, we consider images to be multisensory. Therefore, images include sight, hearing, and the bodily sensations of smell, touch, and taste. The goal of assessing your images is to view past events as an experience of a younger self that bears no implications for you today.

EXERCISE: Assessing Your Images

When you're stressed or anxious, you may experience a combination of thoughts and images. Try your best to identify some of these images. You may have, for example, a mental picture of a body sensation like feeling tight or puffy. Below we'll ask you to respond to some questions. Similar questions have been used by Osman et al. (2004) and Veale and Neziroglu (2010) to assess images in BDD.

Now think about the most recent time when you felt anxious about your appearance (when you weren't looking in a mirror or reflective surface). In light of that experience, answer the following questions. Write your answers in your notebook. Your responses will aid in assessing your images.

- Have you ever experienced images or pictures about how you look when you are anxious about your appearance?

If yes:

- How would you describe those images in your mind?

- Are any of these images recurrent or do any involve the same body part?

- Are they intrusive? Do you ever use the image to mentally check what you look like?

If no:

- If you don't have an actual mental picture, you may still have a feeling about how you think others see you. Has this ever happened to you?

- How often do you experience this feeling? Does it provoke anxiety?

- When was the last time you had a feeling when thinking about your appearance?

- Can you bring this picture or how you felt to your mind now? Try to make it as real as possible.

- What do you see in the picture or what do you feel?

- Is what you see in the mental image the same as what you see in a mirror?

- Are you looking out through your eyes or are you looking *at* yourself?

- Do you check your appearance with this mental image when a mirror is unavailable?

- Do you use the same image, or are there many different images?

Now that you've identified some images and/or feelings, we'd like you to identify your assumptions and beliefs about the imagery. Please answer the questions below.

Let's assume the image or feeling you have of yourself is correct.

- What is the most distressing aspect about this?

- If that were true, what would be so upsetting about it?

- What would that mean about you?

- How strongly do you believe that on a scale from 0 to 10 (0 = don't believe it at all; 10 = believe it completely)?

- If that were true, what would it mean about your relationships with others?

- Do these assumptions represent your current feelings and opinions?

- As you think of the image, how real does the image feel right now on a scale of 0 to 10 (0 = not real at all; 10 = extremely real)?

- How would you rate your anxiety about this image on a scale of 0 to 10 (0 = not at all distressing; 10 = extremely distressing)?

The next step is to make an emotional bridge between the image and past experiences.

- When do you remember first feeling this way?

- Do you associate this with a certain moment or memory?

- Where were you?

- How old were you?

- Was anything significant happening in your life at that time?

- Do you remember how you felt about yourself at that time?

- Do you associate a certain memory from that time with the image?

- If yes, can you try to remember it as vividly as possible and describe it?

- What do you see in the memory?

- What feelings do you notice? Are there any smells? Are you touching anything? Are you doing any specific actions or activities?

- What does this mean about you?

- Is the memory similar to images and emotions you experience today?

Reliving Your Experience

The first stage of assessing your images may overlap with the principles of exposure. The images are usually traumatic and emotionally charged, giving rise to distress and anxiety (Kosslyn et al. 1985; Vrana, Cuthbert, and Lang 1986; Holmes and Mathews 2005). Image rescripting involves reliving the memory from the age it was first experienced. Thus, as you're reliving it, you may feel very uncomfortable, because it's similar to exposure (see chapter 6). You're exposing yourself to images that are unpleasant, just as you did in the exercises in chapter 6. But remember, although you may experience anxiety and distress while doing these exercises, ultimately you'll no longer react to the situation or—in this case—image.

You may choose to reflect on the exercises below by writing in your notebook, or, if you prefer, you may go through the exercises with a friend or family member in whom you feel comfortable confiding.

EXERCISE: Reliving Your Experience

Choose a memory about being teased or bullied or any other unpleasant event. Describe the event in the first person and in present tense. For example, "I am fourteen years old, sitting in the bleachers at my high school's homecoming game." Describe all aspects of your environment: what you see, hear, and feel. The key to this exercise is identifying and understanding the meaning of the event and what you felt at that particular age (for example, as the fourteen-year-old). What would you have wanted to occur during the event? For example, you may have wanted protection from a peer or an adult who was abusive emotionally or sexually.

Try to summarize the meaning of the event to your past self and explore alternative meanings when this event is viewed from an adult perspective. In other words, as an adult, what would you think, how would you handle the situation, how could you make it better, and what is your perspective as you look back on the event?

Repeating and Rescripting Your Memory from an Adult Self-Perspective

After you've considered an alternative meaning of the event from the adult perspective, repeat the memory from the perspective of an adult who is compassionate and understanding toward you in the event. You may choose to be the child self or the adult in certain circumstances, such as in cases of physical and/or sexual abuse. Or you may choose to be an authority figure, a sibling, or even a mythical character.

Always begin the rescripting by naming the part of the self (for example, the child self or the adult self) or the role you're adopting (for example, parent or sibling). Sometimes it can be useful to take the perspective of another person in the rescripting because the adult self may be overly critical of the child self (for example, "She should have stood up in the bleachers and walked away from the situation").

When the exercise is completed, explore the adult or other figure evaluation of the child self. This can aid in updating your body image. If, for example, the adult is critical of the child self, then the body image may remain negative. The idea is to rescript the image so that the adult self protects and understands the child self.

You and your partner can discuss these questions—or reflect on them in your notebook:

- What is your child self feeling and thinking? How would you like to help your younger self?

- Do you think your child self would like to be rescued by an adult? What would your child self like to say to the person who was bullying or harming you? Would you like help from someone? As an adult, what would you tell your child self?

Next, script your memory from the perspective of the younger self but with the help of the adult self—that is, the adult self enters the situation to rescue the younger self. Think about what else the younger self may need to occur to feel better. Consider these questions:

- What would you tell your adult self?

- What more would you like your adult self to say or do?

Use the chart below to track your practice and progress.

IMAGERY PRACTICE CHART

Date/Time	Situation	Imagery Used	Comments

Historical Role Play: An Alternative to Imagery

You may struggle with imagery as a means of exploring alternative meanings. A helpful alternative is to do a historical role-play with a close family member or friend. There are three stages to a historical role-play:

1. Revisiting the original interaction

2. Doing a reverse role play

3. Rescripting the interaction

Let's take a closer look at each of these stages. It's important to actually do the role-play, not just think about it.

REVISING THE ORIGINAL INTERACTION

In revising the original interaction, you play your "younger self" and your partner plays the "other" (for example, a parent or peer involved in the event). Once the role-play is complete, have your partner give you feedback on how accurately you portrayed the character (based on what you told your partner or what your partner may know about that past experience from others). If your partner believes you weren't accurate, she should provide you with corrected or more accurate information; then role-play yourself again. After the role-play, explore your thoughts and emotions triggered by the interaction. Consider these questions:

- What was the worst part of this role-play?

- What emotions did you feel the most intensely?

- What do you think this means about you?

- What do you think this means about your "other"?

- How may this represent the world?

Let's see how this might work for you. Perhaps as a twelve-year-old, you were teased about having thin legs. One day you bought new boots, and you were so happy and proud to wear them even though the boots didn't fit snugly. Some people commented on how nice your boots were and others teased you and said, "Wow, your legs are like sticks!" In the exercise, you play yourself as the twelve-year-old who is being teased; your partner plays the person who teased you. Your partner begins to tease and make comments about your legs, and you either respond or keep quiet. Then let your partner tell you if you actually spoke back at the time (that is, if she knows about the actual event or she knows your character and can guess how you likely would have responded). After the role-play, respond to the questions.

DOING A REVERSE ROLE-PLAY

To do the reverse role-play, you and your partner enter into another interaction. This time your partner is the "younger self" and you are the "other." Try to identify with the other person as much as possible, including that person's emotions and perspective on the situation. For example, your partner plays the twelve-year-old you and you play the one who teases her. Tease your partner about her legs, and keep it up the way you think it was when you were young. Your partner will respond or keep quiet.

When the role-play is finished, explore your emotions and thoughts with these questions:

- As the one who did the teasing, bullying, abusing, or other negative behavior, what emotions do you feel the most intensely?

- What may this mean about you as a person?

- What may this mean about your younger self?

- How may this represent the world?

With the new insight gained by answering these questions, try to formulate an alternative interpretation of the event. By role-playing the original interaction and then doing the role reversal, you experience both how it feels to be teased and how it feels to tease someone. What do you think of the teasing now as an adult? For example, when we've had people do this type of interaction, some conclude, "Everyone is teased. Why did it bother me so much?" Others think, *Wow! Look where I am today. My legs may be thin and that's not so bad; it's better than being fat,* or *I'm so much better off today than I was then. I've had to deal with real tragedies and this was nothing in the scheme of life.*

RESCRIPTING THE INTERACTION

To rescript the interaction, your partner plays the role of the "other" and you play the role of your younger self. Try to rescript the interaction so that you act in new ways. Your partner must try to portray the reaction of the "other" in a convincing way and also respond favorably to your younger self and new behavior.

Hopefully, by rescripting the interaction, you gained a new sense of what took place, experienced different feelings at the time of the interaction, and now feel less vulnerable. As a result of your imagery rescripting, we'd like you to feel and behave differently about that event now as an adult. Let's assume that when you were twelve, you went home and cried and then took off your boots and stared at your legs. From then on, you were so self-conscious about your legs that you wore baggy pants to hide them. With the imagery rescripting, we want you to practice being twelve and telling the other person, "I love my boots and I got a lot of compliments on them" or "Sticks and stones may break my bones, but words will never hurt me." Your partner who plays the teasing friend says something like "Whatever…" and stops teasing and/or continues teasing in a humorous, friendly way.

By doing the exercises in this chapter, you've learned to pay more attention to your environment and to what others are saying as well as to concentrate more on what you're doing. You've learned to get out of your head and into the world, and you've become less preoccupied with your appearance. The imagery rescripting helped change your feelings about events that left scars on you. As an adult, you'll view those events differently and gain more mastery over them. Keep practicing the new behaviors that you've learned in this chapter until you feel you're really out of your head!

8

Acceptance and Commitment Therapy

Living a Valued Life with BDD

While you may have heard of behavioral therapy, cognitive therapy, and exposure and response prevention if you've done any research into treatments for BDD, acceptance and commitment therapy (ACT) is likely new to you. ACT is a type of cognitive behavioral therapy that is based on relational frame theory (RFT), which we discussed in chapter 2. Several studies have shown ACT to be helpful with an array of psychological issues (Hayes et al. 2004). This chapter will introduce you to ACT and how it can help you manage your BDD. For more in-depth information, we suggest the workbook *Get Out of Your Mind and Into Your Life* by Steven Hayes and Spencer Smith (2005).

What Is ACT?

Following the acronym ACT, acceptance and commitment therapy can be defined this way:

Accept what you have, including your struggles with unwanted thoughts, feelings, and sensations—and let them go.

Choose a direction in life that provides a sense of meaning and that follows your values.

Take steps to realize your values and life goals and commit to following through with them (Pearson, Heffner, and Follette 2010).

Acceptance and commitment therapy helps you find a balance between acceptance and change. As psychologist Marsha Linehan puts it, "Acceptance is an active process of self-affirmation rather than passive giving up of constructive and realistic efforts of change" (Linehan 1994). It's accepting past events as unchangeable and being focused on the present. It's recognizing that the body isn't the problem, but rather the problem lies with the desire to escape the body and the feelings that it evokes. For instance, you can try to change your body, which can't always change, or you can focus on some more realistic areas of your life to change. You can also change the mental representation of your body since your image may not be accurate.

Remember Alicia's story? Her concerns about her hair increased significantly after she ended a four-year relationship. Her ex-fiancé quickly moved on from the relationship, leaving Alicia stunned and wondering if he'd already been seeing his new girlfriend while they were still together. Alicia had felt certain that this would be the man with whom she would spend the rest of her life. Confused, she spent a lot of her time pondering what had contributed to the breakup. She had always felt that her hair was a bit "off," but those feelings, which had waned over time, returned when her relationship ended. Alicia felt certain that her "bad hair" had a lot to do with the recent events in her life, so she decided that she was going to fix her hair in order to get her life back on track and start dating again. She isolated herself from family and friends to devote time to this process. She held magazines up to her hair color, comparing models' overall attractiveness to hers, and did research to find the perfect hair color and cut for her face shape and complexion. She also looked up her ex-fiancé's new love interest on a social networking website so she could compare her hair to the new girlfriend's hair and figure out what to fix. When not online, Alicia hunted for the most expensive salons with expert colorists and interviewed them. When she had her hair done, she'd be satisfied with the results for a couple of days, and then she'd usually return to the salon frustrated and claiming that the shade was wrong. While going to salons was her last resort for fixing herself, she finally got to the point where she didn't trust anybody, so she started mixing in-home coloring to create the perfect shade. She also ordered and tried dozens of products to give her hair more volume. To test her products, she had a routine of looking at her hair in various lighting and mirrors and then taking pictures of herself. This arduous process of fixing herself took so much time and effort that she found herself too tired to spend time with friends, leaving her feeling lonely.

You can see that Alicia developed several ways to try to control her looks. Her ultimate goal was to have perfect hair so she'd feel good about herself and finally start dating again. All of these control strategies to change her looks didn't help her accomplish her goal of starting a relationship but actually prevented her from doing so, because she isolated herself and devoted much of her time and energy to her BDD.

If, like Alicia, you use *extreme* ways to control your looks and perceived flaws, one of two things will happen: either your goals are never accomplished as you expect or your efforts take their toll on your confidence, self-esteem, and relationships (Wilson 2004). The ACT techniques that we present in this chapter will help you change the way you view, react to, and interact with your thoughts and feelings.

Pain and Suffering Come Along with Being Human

All humans suffer—it's part of life. There's no way around that because it's normal. Everyone goes through a tough time at one point or another. Everyone experiences psychological pain. Everyone experiences loss and grief. It's an important part of being human. Despite those difficult times, people persevere and continue to love, laugh, and live.

We live in a society that pushes us to be happy all of the time, and it has taught us that we should learn to control negativity. Books, magazines, and television programs are riddled with quick fixes that supposedly will lead us to happiness, just as they are filled with flawless images. You may look at other people and think, *Yeah right, her life is perfect!* But just like you don't broadcast all of your struggles to the world, those "perfect-looking" people don't either.

ACT is about moving from suffering to taking part in life. It's about going forward with your baggage in tow, even though this seems like going backward in light of our culture, which perpetuates the myth of constant happiness and instant gratification. You can't *force* yourself to get rid of your pain, but you can work on it and ACT can help. Treatment isn't always easy, but committing to it can produce the benefit of living a more fulfilling, valued life.

EXERCISE: Just How Old Is Your Problem?

We want you to examine all of the problems that you've been struggling with due to BDD. First, make a list of the problems that your BDD has caused and write them in your notebook.

Now, reflect on these questions and write your responses in your notebook:

- How long have you been struggling?

- Did your problems pop up yesterday? Last month? Last year? Several years ago?

- How have you tried to solve each of the problems you listed?

The problems that you've been dealing with have probably been around for a while, and the way that you've dealt with them may need some tweaking, as your techniques seem to not have been working very effectively. This chapter will help you with that tweaking.

Taking a new perspective on how you approach your BDD can help you change your BDD. By now, you've identified many thought and behavior patterns that are part of your BDD. Because everyone tries to control things that are unpleasant, you've repeatedly tried control strategies that probably have been ineffective. Now we ask you to put those strategies aside and try some new ones. You can't lose anything. You can always go back to your old strategies, if you want.

How Is ACT Different from Cognitive Therapy?

You may be confused by how ACT differs from cognitive therapy. While both focus on ways to manage thoughts, ACT differs in that it doesn't use strategies to alter thoughts or feelings. In ACT, you don't dispute or challenge your thoughts or feelings, nor do you create rational alternatives. Instead, you experience life as it is and accept that. You may wonder why we asked you to learn cognitive therapy if there's a form of therapy that seems to be just the opposite—not to challenge your thoughts. Both approaches have been found to be effective in altering bad feelings. ACT is sometimes very effective when you have a hard time challenging your thoughts or exposing yourself to your fears. ACT gets you started, so to speak. The more tools you have, the better off you are.

Okay, so how can ACT help with your BDD? Sometimes engaging in ERP (exposure and response prevention) can be tough for some people because their pain and suffering is so intense, which makes it too difficult to do exposures in the early stages of treatment. Here are some of the ways that ACT can help with some of those higher-order exposures, the really tough ones:

- Increasing motivation to engage in treatment

- Increasing willingness to experience unwanted thoughts, images, feelings, and situations

- Reducing the tendency of buying into intrusive thoughts

- Targeting values other than appearance

- Living a meaningful existence according to one's values

- Focusing on the present moment

- Accepting unwanted emotions, thoughts, and sensations

- Tolerating symptoms rather than focusing on reducing them

ACT offers a different perspective on how to tackle BDD. (If you're still unclear about the differences between cognitive therapy and ACT after finishing this chapter, go back to chapter 5 and review cognitive therapy.) One of the strengths of ACT is that it shows how language affects how we think and feel, so let's explore that connection now.

The Power of Language

Unlike our animal counterparts, humans have the unique ability of language. Language is quite adaptive. It allows us to connect to each other and live and experience the world in a much different way than animals do. It stimulates complex networks of associated ideas, images, and evaluations. However, language can also lead to much of the psychological suffering humans experience (Hayes and Smith 2005). Let's remember back to chapter 2, which explained language and conditioning. If you don't remember, we suggest you reread the section entitled "Language and Conditioning" before continuing.

Relational frame theory (RFT) posits that our language abilities allow us to represent thoughts, events, ideas, images, evaluations, and memories. Thoughts and words can take on meanings and elicit emotions, including negative ones.

Remember the example about the warm chocolate chip cookies? Well, let's look at some other examples. Hearing certain songs can have a very powerful effect on people. Can you think of a song that transports you back in time or reminds you of a particular person or place? Some songs trigger feelings of happiness and nostalgia if associated with memories of good friends and good times; others trigger feelings of sadness, if that's what you heard during a tough breakup or when someone close to you passed away. Sometimes you don't even need to hear the song; just hearing the artist's name or looking at the album triggers those feelings. And while a song makes one person feel happy because of its associations, that same song evokes heartbreak for another. This illustrates that our minds have the ability to make arbitrary associations—and all we need to reconstruct those associations are our minds.

RFT can help explain how arbitrary relationships impact BDD. For instance, you may have learned that there's a connection between attractiveness or happiness and social and occupational success. If someone comments that your friend is overly sensitive, gets hurt easily, and therefore is hard to talk to, but at the same time she's very pretty, successful, and has people around her all the time, you may arbitrarily connect prettiness and success as well as prettiness and having others tolerate unpleasant attributes. This can then lead you to think, *People tolerate annoying behavior if you're attractive.*

Ultimately, we know that a direct experience with an event isn't needed to develop a response to it. For example, we don't need to touch the stove to know it's hot. We learn not to touch it without enduring a burn. But BDD thoughts and images can be scary and painful, right? And they can make you feel awful, and this can stop you from living your life because you want to avoid reexperiencing that pain. What's really crucial to keep in mind is that these unpleasant internal experiences are *not* harmful. They're a product of our language making arbitrary connections (Hayes and Smith 2005).

You Are Not Your Thoughts

Thoughts create pain. We can conjure up these thoughts 24/7! When you try to control your thoughts or attempt to get rid of them, you actually tend to make things worse. You may have heard this example in some other context:

> Think about elephants—their massive size, grayish color, tough skin, big eyes, long trunks. Picture an elephant taking water into its trunk and spraying itself on a hot day. Now, don't think about elephants. Try your hardest not to think about elephants.

What happened? Did you find yourself thinking about them? Well, that's because when you're thinking about not thinking about something, you are in fact thinking about it! Now let's use a BDD thought as an example. Try this with one of your own thoughts that you identified in chapter 5. We'll use one of Keith's thoughts as a guide.

Keith is insecure about not being muscular enough. He feels anxious and frustrated when he thinks about it, and he thinks about it a lot. The thought *I'm weak* pops into his head throughout the day. He tries to stop it by ignoring the thought or saying to himself *Stop thinking "I'm weak!"* But that makes him think about it all the more.

Now you try it, using the thought you identified. What did you notice?

You may have found that, just as in the "don't think about elephants" example above, when you try not to think about something, you usually end up thinking about it even more. What's the lesson here? Let go of trying to control your automatic thoughts and feelings, and even let go of trying to control your body (Hayes 2004). Why? Because the more you focus on trying to change or control your body or your thoughts, the stronger those thoughts and the desire to control your body appear to be.

Thinking about past and future triggers—events, thoughts, emotions, sensations, and so on—can cause you to avoid anxiety-provoking situations, which makes your BDD worse. If you engage in "coping mechanisms," such as using drugs, you experience even more pain. Ironically, the tools that we use to help ourselves turn into the very traps that we're trying to avoid (Hayes and Smith 2005). It's like getting caught in quicksand—the more you struggle to escape, the more you get stuck and sink.

A thought is just a thought. It is not a fact. You can always find a way to legitimize a thought. And when you start to take these thoughts literally, they cause more struggle. *Cognitive fusion* is when you allow your thoughts to take over and you treat them as truths. With Keith's story, we learned that he was teased about his size in his early teens. He was one of the smaller guys in his class and was pushed around a lot. This didn't just leave him with bumps and bruises—it also left him feeling defeated. These experiences led him to believe *I am physically and mentally weak*. He fused with the label "weak," and now he identifies with that label.

Most of the time, BDD sufferers have responded repeatedly to intrusive thoughts in maladaptive ways. ACT teaches that you can respond differently without changing the form or content of the intrusive thought; this is called *cognitive defusion*. It doesn't get rid of pain, but it teaches you to be in the present moment—noticing thoughts as thoughts and not as facts (Eifert and Forsyth 2005). So if Keith were to do a defusion exercise targeting his thought *I am weak*, he would say, "I am having the thought that I am weak." Simply by prefacing his thought *I am weak* with "I am having the thought that…," Keith creates some distance from his thought; he separates his thought from reality.

Defusion helps you recognize your thoughts as thoughts rather than as facts, which can be very helpful in dealing with your BDD. Let's look at some defusion exercises that you can use.

EXERCISE: Sticks and Stones May Break My Bones, but Words Will Never Hurt Me

You probably recognize the name of this exercise; most of us used these words at some point during childhood. At first, the reason we named this exercise "Sticks and Stones" may not be clear, but stay with us. The meaning will be clear by the time you finish the exercise!

Say "Milk"!

This ACT exercise is commonly known as the "Milk Exercise" (Hayes, Strosahl, and Wilson 1999). What do you think about when you read or hear the word "milk?" Write your thoughts about milk in your notebook before reading ahead.

Our clients' most common answers are "white," "creamy," and "cow." Now, find a private place. We want you to repeat the word "milk" out loud—be sure to say it aloud because saying it in your head doesn't have the same effect—and as fast as you can while still actually pronouncing the word. Do this for thirty to forty-five seconds. Ready, set, go!

So what did you think as you repeated the word? Did "milk" carry the same meaning or images as it did before you did the exercise? What else did you notice? Anything different about the way the word sounded?

What happens most often is that the word "milk" tends to lose its meaning when you repeat it over and over. As you say it, "milk" no longer brings to mind "white and creamy." What's also interesting is that it usually starts to sound strange, too. Sometimes you can't tell where one "milk" ended and where the next began. It becomes gobbledygook!

Say Your Word!

Now let's take this exercise and apply it to BDD. Think of a word that evokes a negative thought or feeling related to your BDD. For example, Keith's word would be "weak." Other BDD words may be "ugly," "acne," "fat," and "short." These are just examples, and we prefer that you find a word that evokes negative thoughts for you.

After you've chosen your word, do the same thing as you did with the word "milk." First, think about the meaning of your word and how it makes you feel. Then write the meaning and your feelings in your notebook. Finally, repeat your word out loud quickly for thirty to forty-five seconds.

How do you feel now? What happened to the word? Research (Masuda et al. 2004) has shown when people do this exercise, they believe in their word less and feel less of an emotional tie to it, despite knowing what the word means. And that brings us back to the title of the exercise. This exercise makes words less like sticks and stones.

We've established that words can sting, especially when we fuse with them. Negative thoughts, emotions, sensations, and memories can be like boomerangs—throw them away and they come right back. Here are a few exercises that can help you defuse from your negative thoughts and feelings. These exercises have been adapted from Steven Hayes and Spencer Smith (2005).

EXERCISE: Switch It Up!

Rather than just having your thoughts, feelings, or sensations go by, label them by saying them out loud. Remember Matthew, who was concerned with his nose? He would often have thoughts like *My nose is awful, I need to have cosmetic surgery,* and *I am disgusting.* So rather than letting those just pass by, he can work on defusing from them by saying the following:

- "I am having the thought that my nose is awful."

- "I am having the thought that I need to have cosmetic surgery."

- "I am having the feeling that I am disgusting."

We would like you to follow suit and do the same. Get out your notebook and write down some examples using these labels:

- "I am having the thought that…"

- "I am having the feeling that…"

- "I am having the sensation that…"

In addition to writing a few examples down, practice using these techniques daily: for maximum benefit, both write them down *and* say them out loud.

Some other ways to deal with BDD negativity include changing how you say your negative thoughts. Sometimes being playful with a BDD thought is a good way to defuse from it. You can do this by

- changing the speed at which you say it—slow it down or speed it up;

- changing your tone of voice—say it like a sports broadcaster or an auctioneer; or

- singing it to a song—choose your favorite song or something silly.

Be creative with how you work on defusing from your thoughts. There's no set way to do it; different strategies work for different people. Now let's move on to another strategy for you to try.

EXERCISE: I Am Not BDD

Another defusion technique is to treat your BDD as an entity separate from you. This technique is similar to the "I am having the thought" exercise. You can work on defusing your thoughts and feelings by saying and writing the following:

- "My BDD is acting up again!"

- "My BDD is saying that…"

- "My BDD is making me feel…"

- "Thank you, BDD, for making me think…"

Oftentimes our clients tell us that thinking about BDD as something separate from them—something they *have* rather than something they *are*—is really helpful. Remember that you are not your thoughts or BDD. With practice, these exercises will help you defuse from your thoughts and feel more empowered.

There are endless thought defusion techniques. Feel free to come up with your own after you have gotten the hang of using the ones in this book. You can combine some of these techniques with your ERP, if you would like. For example, if you're on a roll with these techniques and really want to show BDD who is boss, don't allow it to bully you into doing things: broadcast your negative thoughts and feelings as an exposure, and don't engage in the behaviors that you've done for such a long time.

Stop Living according to How You Feel

Avoiding difficult situations and emotions is like casting a net while fishing. You try to only catch the positive emotions and experiences, but you can't avoid catching some of the negative ones. So what's a better situation? Catching some bad fish with the good and knowing that you'll at least have some good? Or not casting your net to avoid catching the bad? Well, if you avoid casting your net, you're certain to catch nothing—neither good nor bad.

Avoidance is a short-term strategy—a quick fix. We're used to getting "rid" of things we don't like, but this is hard to do with thoughts, memories, and feelings. Back in chapter 2, we addressed the fact that anything can relate to anything else. Our minds have the ability to justify or rationalize anything. Language and our verbal abilities always keep us close to suffering because we can't just turn our suffering off. *Experiential avoidance* is avoiding your experiences, including thoughts, bodily sensations, memories, and behavioral predispositions (Hayes and Smith 2005). We're aware that avoidance may be great in reducing the bad stuff in the short run, but it's a lousy way to manage in the long run because it just makes things worse. If you avoid trigger situations, people, or events, you don't necessarily avoid the difficult feelings connected with them. Why? Because all you need is words to trigger difficult feelings, and words come from your head. Words can conjure up anything!

Mindfulness

Mindfulness is an integral part of ACT. *Mindfulness* is the willingness to experience the moment just as it is. It's being fully present in the moment. It's focusing your attention on what you're experiencing and letting go of your judgments of the experience. It's a way of living, not a goal. It doesn't necessarily mean being okay or feeling good about an experience. It just means being aware of it. This includes being aware of your negative emotions and thoughts. This concept may seem backward to you because you're probably trying to get rid of negative emotions and thoughts. We're all often told that things should be good and happy and perfect and that we should actively try to rid ourselves of what is not. This is not being mindful.

Here's an example of being mindful: Because Alicia has a large extended family, she's frequently invited to weddings of relatives. In the past these events were bittersweet for her; she'd be happy for the couple but couldn't help thinking about her own love life, which left her feeling sad and lonely. Consequently, she began to make excuses in order to avoid attending family functions. But then, to practice being more mindful, Alicia intentionally chose to accept every wedding invitation she received. She still had some negative thoughts from time to time, but rather than leaving the wedding or getting rid of her thoughts, she became aware of her judgments and consciously didn't try to change them.

By being mindful, Alicia was able to overcome some of her feelings of loneliness and isolation. She reconnected with some family members who've been great social support for her. And by tolerating her judgments and feelings and not avoiding these gatherings, Alicia learned that people really didn't care about her appearance as much as she thought they did.

Sometimes people think of mindfulness as just a form of relaxation or as a distraction, but it isn't, as you can see in the example from Alicia's life above. Being mindful requires practice, a lot of it. Thousands of thoughts bombard us all, making it easy to fall prey to irrational thoughts and to let these irrational thoughts guide our interpretations of reality.

A good way to practice mindfulness is to include it in everyday activities, especially activities that we often neglect or don't even think about—breathing, eating, and being in our bodies. Let's look at these activities now.

Mindfulness and Breathing

Breathing, of course, is an essential part of life. While we all breathe constantly, starting at birth and continuing throughout life, our breathing varies. It changes according to what we're doing and how we feel. Sometimes we forget about breathing and don't pay attention to it because it's always there. Do you ever pay attention to your breathing during different activities such as walking upstairs, lying in bed before you fall asleep, or before speaking or performing in front of an audience? How about while experiencing different emotions? Ever notice how your breathing changes when you're excited or nervous?

Breathing is an important component in mindfulness (Kabat-Zinn 1990). Working with your breathing allows you to focus on its ever-changing nature and to be comfortable with your breathing's potential to change. To breathe mindfully, focus on breathing from your stomach, or what's called "abdominal" or "diaphragmatic breathing." With this kind of deep breathing, focus on your abdomen expanding, filling with breath. This takes a bit of time to learn. One way that you can tell that you're doing deep breathing is to put your hand on your abdomen and be aware of it going up and down. When you inhale, your abdomen should expand and your hand should rise up; when you exhale, your abdomen should contract and your hand should go down.

We provide a few exercises below to help you become more mindful, including being more mindful of your breathing. Again, we must emphasize that being mindful takes daily practice. These exercises can help you on your way.

EXERCISE: Mindful Breathing

How about giving mindful breathing a try? Read through the exercise once so you know what the exercise involves—or have someone you trust read the exercise to you as you do it.

In a quiet place, get into a comfortable position, either sitting or lying down. Close your eyes. Or if that makes you feel uncomfortable, pick a neutral point (like the wall) to gaze upon in an unfocused way. Now breathe in through your nose and out through your mouth. Pay attention to your breath, but don't manipulate it. Notice it coming into your nose and escaping from your mouth. Notice your lungs filling. Notice your chest going up and down. Notice your abdomen rising as you breathe in and falling as you breathe out. Feel your lungs expand and contract. Be aware of your breathing. If you notice that your awareness wanders off or judgmental thoughts nudge their way in, just bring your mind back to your breath. Do this for five minutes.

As we mentioned, being mindful takes some work. We hope that you can become more in touch with your breathing on a daily basis. We ask that you work on this until it feels like second nature. Start off with five minutes for the first couple of days and then increase it to ten minutes.

Eventually, we'd like you to feel comfortable enough to increase your mindful breathing to fifteen minutes per day.

Mindfulness and Eating

Like breathing, eating is essential. People spend a lot of time figuring out what they're going to eat, buying food, preparing it, going out to eat, and then actually eating and digesting food. People have different relationships with food. Eating different things makes us feel differently. For example, compare eating ice cream to eating cottage cheese. You may like one, both, or neither. When we mentioned ice cream and cottage cheese, you may have thought of an experience you had with ice cream or cottage cheese—a fond memory from childhood or maybe the thought that ice cream is a fattening food and cottage cheese isn't. You may feel disgusted thinking about the consistency and smell of cottage cheese. Or you may feel anxious thinking of the calories in ice cream. People tend to fall into traps of judging experiences with food, especially in a society that promotes being very thin.

Today we're accustomed to eating on the go. We may eat in the car or in front of the television; we may have lunch during class or a business meeting. Unfortunately, for this reason, we tend not to pay attention to what and why we're eating. When you eat, do you eat out of hunger, boredom, or stress? Because food can taste so good, some people fall into the trap of coping with their emotions by using food. Not only is this a way of coping with emotions, it can also be a way of avoiding them altogether.

We want you to pay attention to what and why you're eating. Being mindful of your eating can make it a more enjoyable experience. The exercise below will introduce you to mindful eating.

EXERCISE: Eating Mindfully

To do this exercise, you'll need a mint or a small piece of chocolate. Find a quiet place where you can sit comfortably and follow the steps below.

1. Hold the mint. Don't put it in your mouth yet. There's a lot to experience first. What comes to mind when you think of mints? Allow these

thoughts to come and go, not judging them. What does the mint feel like in your hand? Note its shape, texture, and color. Some mints feel smooth and others feel chalky. Some leave a residue on your fingers or some color from the dye if it begins to melt.

2. Smell the mint. What's it smell like? Can you tell its flavor just by holding it up to your nose?

3. Put it in your mouth, but don't chew on it. Feel it with your tongue and roll it around your mouth. Pay attention to how it dissolves and changes shape. What does it taste like? How is the consistency?

4. Now chew the mint and experience your feelings. Notice your muscles around your mouth as you chew the mint. Is the mint soft or hard?

5. Now swallow the mint. Feel it going down.

Reflect on the experience. How did eating the mint feel? Did you notice anything different from your usual experience of eating? Usually, people become aware of just how unaware they are when they're eating. Did you pay attention to how long the process took? Was your inclination to put more than one mint in your mouth? People often eat really quickly or put too much food in their mouths to really experience it mindfully. When was the last time you ate popcorn one kernel at a time? When you practice eating mindfully, eat one piece at a time or use a smaller fork or spoon.

Now that you've mindfully eaten a mint, try eating one meal mindfully each day. We all often judge food when we eat, but we want you not to judge what you're eating. Also, it's preferable that you eat with minimal distraction—don't eat while driving or watching television. Incorporate all of your senses while eating and focus in on your feelings of hunger and fullness.

Mindfulness and Your Body

As a society, we're hyperfocused on the way we look. How we think about our bodies gets in the way of us being comfortable in them. We want you to just experience your body for all the things it allows you to do, not how you feel it holds you back (because that is a judgment). For the last mindful exercise below, we'd like you to practice being in your skin in a nonjudgmental way. We acknowledge that can be hard due to your BDD. You may feel uncomfortable in your skin, wish you had a different body, or wish you had a different particular body part. But that's okay. Just be aware of your thoughts and feelings, and then let them go.

EXERCISE: Being Mindful of Your Body

This mindful exercise is known as a body scan. You focus on the sensations of each part of your body (Kabat-Zinn 1990). Find a quiet place to lie down, but stay alert—don't fall asleep, because that defeats the purpose of the exercise. Read through the exercise once so you know what the exercise involves. Or, if you prefer, make a recording of it or have someone you trust read the exercise to you as you do it. If you notice judgmental thoughts surfacing while you do the exercise, especially when you focus on a body part that you may find flawed, just take a breath and refocus your attention on the sensations in your body. Follow these steps:

1. Pay attention to your breath. Take a few deep breaths and get comfortable.

2. Start off by focusing on the feeling in your toes. You can wiggle them a bit if you want. Feel the sensations in your toes. Focus on the feeling. If you feel nothing, that's okay—just focus on that.

3. Now take a deep breath before transitioning to the next body part (see list below). Repeat steps 1 through 3 for each body part, in the order given.

    - Feet

    - Lower legs/calves

    - Upper legs/thighs

    - Pelvis

    - Abdomen/lower back

- Chest/upper back

- Shoulders

- Hands

- Arms

- Shoulders again

- Neck

- Head

- Face

4. When you have gone through all of the body parts, focus on your body as a whole for about five minutes.

Reflect on the experience. Did you notice parts of your body that you never really paid attention to before? Did you find it hard to concentrate on each body part? Did your thoughts take you away from the experience? Did you feel relaxed or tense?

===

Judgmental thoughts may have attempted to make their way in while you were doing the body scan, especially while you were focused on a body part that you may find flawed. If and when that occurs as you do this exercise in the future, just take a breath and refocus on the sensations. Mindfulness is experiencing these thoughts and feelings in a nonjudgmental way.

Living toward Your Values, Not Your Looks

Imagine that you have a ball and chain attached to your ankle. You don't have the key, and you need to be somewhere—somewhere that you've really wanted to be for a very long time. Imagine what that place might be for you. Maybe you're on your way to see a movie or a band that you love, or to see your child being born, or to visit with your favorite person. Now that you have something in mind, let's go. Oh, wait! You still have that ball and chain around your ankle. You look around, and nobody's there to help you. You shout and nobody hears you. Time is ticking. So what do you do? Here are some options:

a. Wait for someone to come to you and see if he can find the key.

b. Start moving, drag that ball and chain and look back at them every minute or so to yell and glare at them.

c. Pick up the ball and chain and carry them.

Choose one. With option A, you don't know if or when someone will show up to help. And if someone does, he may not have the key or be strong enough to cut the chain, even if he has the right tools with him. Moving onto option B: What's the point of giving a dirty look at the ball and chain or yelling at them? They're a ball and chain! They can't see or hear you anyway. While this option allows you to move about, you spend a lot of time stopping and engaging the ball and chain in conversation. That just slows you down. And then there's option C: The ball and chain may be a bit heavy, but if you pick them up and get moving, at least you'll get to where you want to be. Okay, it may not be as fast as you'd like, but at least you'll get a chance to experience that great occasion. If you stay behind waiting for the key, you won't get anywhere. So rather than waiting for that ball-and-chain BDD (or any other pain, for that matter) to go completely away, live life according to what you most deeply value.

If you allow yourself to experience your negative thoughts and emotions rather than avoiding them—that is, if you pick up your ball and chain and move toward what's important to you—you'll be able to live a more fulfilling life. We acknowledge that doing this is difficult. If it wasn't hard, you probably would have done it by now. To help you pick up your "ball and chain" and move toward what's important to you, let's take a closer look at what you most deeply value. The following exercises will help you explore your *values*—what is important to you and what makes your life worth living.

EXERCISE: Life without BDD

Imagine that you aren't plagued with worries and concerns about your looks. What would your life be like? What would you focus on? What would your day-to-day life look like? How would work or school be different? And relationships? What about hobbies?

Take some time, about fifteen minutes, and just envision what your life would look like if you didn't have BDD. We acknowledge that you may find it difficult to think about life without thinking about your appearance. Pretend that a genie just granted you the wish that your BDD is gone. It may help to close your eyes and really envision what your life would look like—minute by minute, hour by hour, day by day. Jot these down in your notebook under the heading "Life without BDD."

Now compare this life without BDD to life with it. Write these observations in your notebook under the heading "Life with BDD."

Here's an example of Ana's life with BDD and how she envisions her life without BDD:

Life with BDD	*Life without BDD*
• Skip classes because I'm too embarrassed by the way I look	• Attend classes and not care or think about the way I look
• Can't concentrate when in class because I keep thinking about the way I look	• Do well in my classes and have a 3.5 GPA or higher
• Isolate myself from friends	• Hang out with my old friends and meet new people at school
• Avoid meeting new people	• Be social and go to parties
• Feel lonely	• Go to church services and not care if people look at me

- Avoid going to church services because I'm too embarrassed by the way I look, so I can't pay attention, which makes me feel guilty

- Join a religious club on campus

Now take a look at both of your lists. How are they similar? How are they different?

We asked you to reflect on your lists because they probably contain some hints as to what your values are. We'll revisit your values in a bit, but before we do that, here's another helpful exercise. We know this may seem dark, but this exercise is extremely beneficial for examining your values.

EXERCISE: New York Times Obituary

Please write your own obituary in your notebook. Describe your character, qualities, and accomplishments.

Sometimes we find it helpful to look backward, say from death, because it gives us a different perspective on life. Examining how you hypothetically lived in an obituary can help give you a fresh outlook on how you want to live your life now.

How did you feel writing this? How you write about your life is a good indicator of your values. Look back at what you wrote. What do you want your life to be about?

Discovering Your Values

Earlier in this chapter, we defined a *value* as what is most important to you. Despite values being different from person to person, the things that people find important and meaningful tend to fall under these categories (adapted from Michelle Heffner and Georg Eifert [2004]):

- **Career.** What you do for a living.

- **Citizenship/Volunteerism.** Helping others—going to the homeless shelter to serve meals, being a mentor, running a race or doing a walk for a cause, and so on.

- **Education.** Being involved in higher or continuing education—going to college, taking an extracurricular course, participating in an adult education program (for example, bird watching, woodworking, current events), taking part in other educational opportunities.

- **Health and Well-Being.** Taking care of yourself—eating healthy, working out, going to yoga classes, and so on.

- **Leisure and Hobbies.** What you do for fun and in your spare time—taking pictures, singing, playing sports, cooking, and so on.

- **Relationships—Family.** This includes your family members (aside from your romantic partner)—parents, grandparents, siblings, cousins, and so on.

- **Relationships—Friends.** Relationships with nonrelatives—people from work, church, school, and so on.

- **Relationships–Intimate.** Romantic relationships—significant other, boyfriend, girlfriend, partner, or spouse.

- **Spirituality/Religion.** What you believe in—praying daily, being with nature, chanting, going to services, and so on.

The next exercise will help you explore these value categories to find what's most important to you. You'll need your notebook, so have it ready.

EXERCISE: What Really Matters to You?

Find a quiet place where you won't be interrupted. Review the categories and write them in your notebook, leaving some space after each category. If there's a category missing that you value (other than your looks), please add it to the end of the list in your notebook. Think about each of these areas of your life and what your corresponding values are. Write them down in your notebook. Remember, values are what are meaningful to you.

Once you've determined what your values are, you can then explore how much you follow—and how much you'd like to follow—those values. The exercise below will guide your exploration.

EXERCISE: How Much Do You Follow Your Values?

Now that you've identified your values, we'd like you to consider how much you follow your values in your life *now* as well as how much you'd like to follow them in your *ideal life*. Let's start by looking at how much you follow your values currently.

How Much Do You Follow Your Values Now?

Review the value categories in the worksheet below. Think about why these values are important to you. Reflect on how much time and effort you put into meeting these values. Then rate the value categories by how you live your life *now*, using a 1 to 10 scale (1 = not living up to or dedicating much time to the value; 10 = living fully up to or dedicating a lot of time to the value). All of the categories represent positive things since values are what are important to people, so don't rate everything a 9 or 10. Be honest with yourself about what's most important to *you*. Write your ratings in the column titled "How I Live Life Now," or, if you prefer, you can sketch the table in your notebook and place your ratings there.

VALUES

Value Category	How I Live Life Now	How I Would Ideally Live Life	Discrepancy
Career			
Citizenship/ Volunteerism			
Education			
Health and Well-Being			
Leisure and Hobbies			
Relationships– Family			
Relationships– Friends			
Relationships– Intimate			
Spirituality/Religion			

How much you live your life according to your values affects how satisfied you feel with your life. That makes sense, right? If there are relationships or activities that are really important to you but you don't nurture those relationships or engage in those activities, then you probably won't feel complete or satisfied.

How Much Would You Follow Your Values in Your Ideal Life?

Now rate your values based on the life you envisioned in the "Life without BDD" exercise (above), your ideal life. Again, use the 1 to 10 scale. Write these ratings in the column "How I Would Ideally Live Life."

Next, category by category, subtract column 1 ("How I Live Life Now") from column 2 ("How I Would Ideally Live Life") and write that number in the "Discrepancy" column.

How Ana Follows Her Values

Before we take a closer look at your ratings, let's see how Ana rated her value categories. Ana didn't have any other value categories to add, but you should add categories to the end of your list if you feel as if something (aside from your looks) is missing.

ANA'S VALUES

Value Category	How I Live Life Now	How I Would Ideally Live Life	Discrepancy
Career	3	7	4
Citizenship/ Volunteerism	2	2	0
Education	3	7	4
Health and Well-Being	3	3	0
Leisure and Hobbies	.7	5	–2
Relationships– Family	8	8	0
Relationships– Friends	2	6	4
Relationships– Intimate	1	7	6
Spirituality/Religion	4	9	5

Compare Ana's two columns. We assume that they aren't identical because everyone has discrepancies between their real and ideal lives. As you can see with Ana's values above, the numbers don't all match up. That means that she isn't living her life now according to her values. There are rather sizable differences in many value categories. While her largest discrepancy is with intimate relationships—Ana would like to get married in the future—she's not looking for that type of relationship at the moment and would like to focus on the other discrepancies. Other categories to address include spirituality/religion, friendships, education, and career. For Ana, education and career are interrelated because she'd like to go to medical school and become a doctor.

If you look at her chart again, you can see that Ana has a few areas where she's currently living up to her ideals (as designated by a discrepancy of 0). Her family relationships are extremely important to her, and despite her BDD, she's very invested in maintaining those relationships.

You may have noticed that Ana scored a negative discrepancy in the leisure and hobbies category. This means that she's devoting more of her time to this value than she would like. While she really enjoys painting and watching movies, she's been doing them more often than usual while avoiding other meaningful activities that she feels she can't do because of her BDD.

How You Follow Your Values

Now look at your own ratings. What are the differences that you notice? Where are your values discrepant? We think that, if you start to live a more valued life, you'll start feeling better about yourself, even if your appearance does not change.

In the exercise below, you'll take a look at some of your values where you found a difference between how you're living your life now and how you want to live your life. In order to live a more value-driven life, you'll need to break those down into steps or goals. These steps should be realistic and attainable. As you do this, also look at the values that you rated the same in your real and ideal life. What makes you feel as if you're accomplishing something in those categories? Your answer may provide a clue to doing the same with other categories that you value.

EXERCISE: Working toward Your Values by Establishing Goals

As we have already specified, values aren't the same as goals. Values are what are most important to you, and *goals* are manageable tasks that you can do or actions you can take that lead toward your values. For instance, your family is something that you probably value, but family isn't a goal. A goal that would help fulfill the value category of family may be everyone sitting down to dinner together without interruptions at least four times a week. To summarize, values are directions and goals are destinations (Eifert and Forsyth 2005). Values are the compass that guides how we want to live our lives; they provide direction. Goals are the destinations where we stop along our journey.

Please identify at least five short-term and five long-term goals that can help you toward more valued living. As in the list of treatment goals that you made in chapter 4, please articulate specific, doable goals. To help you along, here's an illustration of Ana's goals for working toward her values.

Ana's Short-Term Goals

- Return to college (education).

- Initiate spending time with close friends twice a week (friendships).

- Begin daily prayers and attending services every week (spirituality/religion).

Ana's Long-Term Goals

- Go to medical school (education).

- Go to social gatherings where I can meet new people (friendships).

- Go to an impoverished area for one year to do missionary work and volunteer medical services (spirituality/religion).

Now that you've established some value-driven goals, work on making them happen. Sometimes goals need to be broken down into smaller steps to make them more doable. For example, after Ana graduates from college (one of her short-term goals), she wants to attend medical school. The process of applying to and getting into medical school is arduous. Some of the smaller steps in this process are to look for schools that would be a good fit, take the MCAT, fill out applications, and go to interviews. Now break your goals down into smaller, doable steps.

Whenever you meet your goals and check them off your list, make a new list. When you use your values to set goals in life, you'll find it's easier to pursue and meet those goals, which will lead you toward living a more fulfilling life.

As we've seen in this chapter, the goal of ACT is to live according to your values rather than living in the service of your BDD, leading to a more meaningful existence. ACT is

Accepting your thoughts and your feelings

Choosing a path that follows what really matters

Taking active steps to realize your goals and values

Remember, living life to its fullest means accepting everything that comes with it—the good, the bad, and the perceived ugly.

9

How Do You
Prevent Relapse?

*G*ive yourself a well-deserved pat on the back. You're almost all the way through this book, and hopefully you're continuing to identify and address your thoughts and systematically alter your behavior. Maybe you can wear a short-sleeved shirt to a friend's barbecue without worrying that everyone is staring at your arms. Maybe you no longer feel anxious when you run an errand without putting on makeup. You should be proud of any progress you have made, because it means that you've worked hard to enrich your own well-being. So, what now? Does that mean it's time to close this book and forget your difficulties along with the treatment you've used to combat them? The truth is that it requires work to maintain the goals you've reached.

Why Relapse Occurs

Despite the tremendous impact that cognitive behavioral therapy can have on BDD, relapse can occur for a variety of reasons. For example, you may stop practicing what you learned and go back to old habits; you may have stopped reading through the book once you achieved a certain level of success, or perhaps a stressor (such as a death in the family) or a life transition (such as graduating, getting married, or becoming a parent) makes you susceptible to reexperiencing BDD symptoms. Life goes on after the book and all your hard work, so you can't rest on your laurels and think all will go smoothly thereafter.

Can you anticipate some reasons why you might stop practicing what you learned? Try to come up with three reasons and write them in your notebook.

As we said, relapse can occur for a number of reasons. It's most likely to occur when you become so comfortable with your gains that you begin to neglect your exercises. Now, don't get us wrong, we want you to feel excited, proud, and ecstatic about the gains you've made, because you certainly deserve it! But sometimes the boredom of practicing your exercises over and over again may lead you to think *I don't need these stupid exercises anymore. Maybe they used to help me, but I am beyond that now, so continuing to do ERP, cognitive therapy, attentional training, or ACT would be a colossal waste of time.* This is a trap. BDD is something that can be managed, but unfortunately it's not a disorder that will disappear and never return. Managing it requires continuous effort until it no longer seems like effort. Neglecting your exercises is the easiest way to ensure a relapse.

For someone who has dealt with terrible anxiety for years, even a small improvement can feel incredible, but we implore you not to stop there. Keep working until you can do your ERP exercises with ease and continue to come up with new exercises; doing that makes it less likely that you will experience severe anxiety again in the future. If the key to successful CBT is engagement in the various exercises we described in this book, then the key to remaining a success story after treatment is maintaining your gains.

Why Is It Important to Maintain Treatment Goals?

Although some people may remain symptom-free after successfully diminishing their BDD, this is not true for everyone. You may find that—even if your symptoms have decreased and your life has become more functional and enjoyable after months of hard work—giving in to your thoughts, emotions, and behaviors can lead to a downward spiral. However, even if this is not the case and you feel great, you can maintain your gains and even continue to improve. In addition to improvement in your BDD symptoms, if you actively work to maintain your treatment goals, you'll also experience lower levels of anxiety and depression. Push yourself to face your fear head on. Also, regular contact with a therapist or supportive friend is useful in reviewing how you're doing and in modifying your treatment approach as necessary.

Signs of Relapse

At this point, it's important to distinguish between a lapse and a relapse. We define a *lapse* as a temporary setback in which you may experience one or more symptoms, but your symptoms are not as severe as when you first began working on your BDD. Situations you were able to deal with in the past all of a sudden seem like a challenge. Your initial response is to avoid the situation. For example, maybe your BDD was related to your freckles on your arms and legs and you never wore anything but long-sleeved shirts and pants. After a day at the beach, you begin to feel that the exposure to the sun has greatly increased the amount of freckles on your arms, and your anxiety starts to creep up again. Maybe you even make an excuse not to go out with your friend the next day, when the sun is equally strong. In such a situation it's important to counter the lapse with ERP exercises. In other words, call up your friend and say, "My plans fell through; I'd love to hang out tomorrow." Don't let BDD take over your life again. If you begin to make excuses and avoid situations that used to cause you anxiety, you may be heading for a relapse.

A *relapse* can be distinguished from a lapse in that it's almost a full return to your BDD symptoms at the severity you experienced before you picked up this book or sought treatment. To make sure this doesn't happen to you, it's essential that you use your ERP exercises. If some of them seem too daunting, start with exercises that are lower on your hierarchy and work your way up. So if you aren't feeling up to going to the beach for a full day with your friends, opt to meet some friends for lunch at a café with an outdoor section. But if these ERP exercises, which you were once able to do with ease, now seem impossible, begin rereading the book and get yourself motivated again. Ask a friend, a family member, or a therapist to help you out. *Do not* view this as a failure on your part! Unfortunately, it's all too easy to experience a relapse. This is just as true with BDD as with any other challenge you might approach. If your friend was on a diet and he lapsed and ate three doughnuts, would you tell him that his diet was over and that any future attempts to lose weight would be futile? Of course not. So cut yourself some slack and congratulate yourself for recognizing that you're beginning to slip and may need some temporary additional support. In two research studies, we found that relapses could be prevented by continued practice of exposure and cognitive therapy as well as all the other strategies we suggest throughout the book (McKay et al. 1997; McKay 1999). Even two years later our clients who continued to practice relapse prevention improved. Continue to go forward!

Do you think you lapsed or relapsed? What signs of lapse or relapse have you observed? If you relapsed, write down what makes you think that you did in your notebook.

Relapse Prevention: Let's Get Started

Now that you know how to recognize the signs of a lapse or relapse, how do you go about making sure that it doesn't happen to you? The first step is to plan ahead. Once you feel that you've managed to get your BDD symptoms under control, be sure to congratulate yourself, but also remember that though you've gotten over the hump, your journey isn't over. To maintain the gains you've made and to continue to feel better about yourself, you must commit to using the skills you've learned so well. In order to show your commitment to this goal, it's a good idea to draw up a contract for yourself. Does this seem a little silly? Don't roll your eyes, because signing a contract stating the expectations you have for yourself makes you more likely to live up to them.

Here is a sample contract written by Ana, whose BDD revolves around facial blemishes:

SAMPLE CONTRACT

In order to maintain the gains I have made regarding my BDD symptoms:

1. I will continue to practice ERP exercises on a daily basis, going through items on my hierarchy from easier items to harder ones. I will generate additional creative exposures to challenge myself and decrease my BDD symptoms.

2. I will not avoid public places or engaging in conversations with members of the opposite sex.

3. I will challenge my thoughts.

4. I will recognize that my thoughts are just thoughts and are outside of me.

5. I will stick to my values and behave according to my values.

6. I will practice task concentration and attention to my environment.

7. I will evaluate how I'm doing at the end of each week and be honest with myself if I notice that I'm regressing.

8. I will contact my therapist, a family member, or a friend in cases of emergency or if I begin to experience lapses on a frequent basis.

Signature:

Date:

Create a contract like this for yourself. If you've been seeing a therapist, ask your therapist to sign it as well and to check in with you from time to time to ensure that you remain motivated and on track. After you've created and signed this contract, it's time to make sure you have a hierarchy of anxiety-provoking situations. Don't just refer back to the original hierarchy that you created when you first started working on your BDD. Remember, you've made great strides and this list may be irrelevant to you now. Embrace this opportunity to recognize how far you've come and to make even more gains through a new hierarchy. If you're uncertain as to how anxiety-provoking you will find specific situations, assign a tentative SUDS level (see chapter 6), or, even better, test out a situation to discover firsthand how it will make you feel.

Once you have your hierarchy in place, you can move on to the crux of the maintenance program: ERP, cognitive therapy, ACT, task concentration. Start slowly. This is no time to rush. Just as you did with your original hierarchy, start by selecting items with lower SUDS values and expose yourself to these situations until you're bored. Only then should you move up to higher-anxiety items. Whenever you're engaging in ERP exercises, try to assess your anxiety level and any feelings or thoughts you may be experiencing. If you notice that you're having thoughts that interfere, it may be a good time to review cognitive therapy skills (chapter 5).

Having a little bit of a backslide into your old thoughts and behaviors can be expected, so be honest with yourself about the signs of relapse. Stick to your contract. Even when you're symptom free, test yourself by doing some old ERP exercises to ensure that you've maintained your treatment gains.

10

How Can Your
Family Help?

When you read the title of this chapter, maybe you thought *I don't want my family involved in anything.* That's a natural reaction, for several possible reasons: you may be embarrassed to talk about your concerns, you haven't even shared with them how you feel about yourself, they don't understand, you're afraid they'll intrude into your life, or maybe they're already too involved and you want them out of your hair.

Whatever the case may be, your family *is* there, and directly or indirectly they're going to be involved. What do we mean by that? Families have a way of knowing when a member of the family isn't functioning at an optimal level. They witness your struggles, whether you verbalize them or not. They may choose to give you room initially, but if they notice that your struggles worsen, they may be a good resource for you.

What Should You Share with Your Family?

You can choose to share all or very little with your family. How and what you share depends on the nature of your relationship. Even within the same household, you may have certain members with whom you're closer than others. You may have a sister or brother with whom you share things and another sibling that you hardly speak to. You may have an understanding and supportive parent or spouse, or ones that are critical and lack empathy. Choose what you want to share and with whom you want to share it. You may choose to say that you're unhappy with your looks and see how they respond. Most likely they'll say, "Oh gosh, everyone is unhappy with their looks these days." Of course, they're probably responding to our culture's normal discontent, which we spoke about in earlier chapters. You need to emphasize that you aren't talking about what everyone feels, but about something much more serious. You'll need to explain how your preoccupation interferes with your daily life. However, before you spill the beans, if you haven't done so already, write down with whom you're going to share your secret and what you're willing to share.

Here are some examples of how to explain BDD to your loved ones:

- I am very upset by the way I look.

- I am so upset by the way I look that I think about it all day long.

- I look at the mirror throughout the day and I can't stop myself.

- I want to get plastic surgery.

- I hate going out because of the way I look.

- I don't think I can pull it off any longer at work (school).

- I'm afraid you'll reject me if you know how much time I spend on my looks.

- I hate myself. I'm afraid you'll think I'm just vain.

- I'm so afraid you'll criticize me for the way I feel.

- I'm afraid you'll lie to me and tell me I look fine just to make me feel better.

- I don't think I can do anything with my life until my appearance changes.

- I always hated how you compared me to _____.

- I think my sister is so much prettier.

- I think my brother is so much better built than me that I can't stand him.

- I know you want me to work (go to school full-time), but I can't.

- You never understood how I felt about my _____ (area of concern).

- I think I have body dysmorphic disorder.

Think of other things you might want to share—or not share. You may be willing to share a little at a time, depending on how your loved ones respond. Don't forget, this is a whole new way of thinking for them.

What Do You Want from Your Family?

When you share your distress and preoccupation with your family, you should have in mind what it is you want from them. Remember Ana from the introduction? She wanted her parents to take her to dermatologists and to buy the prescribed treatments. Since she was only eighteen, she needed financial and emotional support. She needed to have her parents understand why she wasn't going away to college and why she was so anxious all the time. Keith needed his friends to understand why he wasn't hanging out with them as much and why he spent his whole time at the gym. BDD plagued Matthew's life for a long time. He didn't want his wife to know the extent of his concerns and shared very little with her. However, despite his unwillingness to share, his behaviors clearly indicated a problem and eventually he divorced. Of course, BDD wasn't the only problem in the marriage; in fact, his BDD got much worse after the divorce. Throughout his life, he had issues that impacted his family members in different ways. He shared very little, kept to himself, and felt lonely and ultimately suicidal. Alicia had a hard time dating. She felt more intimidated when she got close to someone. She never got close enough to share her worry about her appearance. The only people with whom she shared her concern about her hair were her parents—and one friend. Her parents were always understanding and emotionally supportive.

Now try making a list of what you want from your family, friend, or spouse. Here are a few examples, but you may think of your own as well.

- Understanding

- Empathy

- To not invite people to the house

- To not be angry when I'm late

- To pay for cosmetic surgery

- To pay for dermatologists

- To pay for products (that is, hair or face products, clothes, prescriptions)

- To stop asking me to socialize

- To allow me to use the bathroom to my heart's content

- To stop comparing me to others

- Other _____

Once you know what you want, it's easier to ask and to let your family know your expectations. Although some of these wants, such as financial support for surgery, may be on your mind, please keep in mind that surgery for BDD has been shown to have negative effects. Now that you've read most of this book, you might also notice that some other items on the list may not be helpful in your recovery. But we do recognize that the recovery process involves some ups and downs. If you're having a difficult day with increased urges to mirror check, communicate this to your family. Explain that you need some space today, but you're willing to accept their help tomorrow to resist mirror checking.

Despite your attempts to educate and express your needs to your family, be prepared for a variety of responses from them. They may resist providing you with some types of support and be confused on whether to accommodate others. Honest and open conversations can help resolve some of the conflict.

What If Your Family Doesn't Understand?

It's true that not all families, friends, or spouses are the same. Everyone's reaction may be different. Try not to be discouraged initially. BDD is a fairly new area, and it hasn't been discussed a lot in the media; therefore, most people don't know about it. If you were to say you're depressed or anxious, most people would know what you were talking about; depression and anxiety are so widely discussed and everyone knows someone who is or has been depressed or anxious. This isn't the case with BDD. It isn't because few people have BDD; we suspect many more people suffer from BDD than is currently estimated. You are not alone by any means. BDD is still in the closet, so to speak.

If your family trivializes your BDD, then explain how much it affects your life. If your family thinks you're narcissistic or vain, explain that it's actually the opposite—you don't like the way you look. If your family thinks you're making excuses not to go to work or school, explain how much time you spend thinking about your looks and how much these thoughts get in the way of your functioning. If your family dismisses your BDD, explain that it's not going away, that it's serious. If you've considered suicide, share that with them. If they say they've never heard of BDD, give them this book to read, tell them to look it up on the Internet, and tell them there are specialists who treat it. (Chapter 4 addresses how to find BDD specialists.) If all fails, then you may find comfort from chat rooms for BDD, a friend, this book, and a therapist.

How Can You Handle Your Anger toward Your Family?

Anger can be a destructive emotion. It can lead to negativity, create discomfort, and breed more anger. Anger affects our immune system and makes us vulnerable to various illnesses. Most of all, it doesn't solve our problem.

If you're angry with your friends, family, or spouse, you need to know why. Here are some reasons that some of our clients have reported to us. Check off those that apply to you.

_____ My parents caused my BDD. They put a lot of emphasis on looks.

_____ My friend keeps comparing one person to another.

_____ My parents judge others based on looks.

_____ After I revealed my darkest inner secret, they took it lightly.

_____ They told others about my appearance concerns.

_____ They don't respect how I feel.

_____ My friends laugh each time I look at my reflection.

_____ My sister is so much better looking than me.

_____ Some people can just go out without makeup or fixing their hair.

_____ I hate my life and those around me.

_____ They refuse to pay for surgery.

_____ No one understands how I feel.

_____ They think they can shut me up by reassuring me.

_____ Other reasons: _____

_____

_____

_____

Once you identify what you're angry about, then you can challenge your thinking, as you learned to do in chapter 5. You want to see how reasonable your anger is. Then come up with a logical, rational way to view your thoughts. After that, you may choose to discuss a possible solution with the person with whom you're angry.

Some family members and friends can be great allies in your fight against BDD; however, they can only help you if they're informed. If you decide that you want to share with them and just don't know how, start off with suggesting that they read the first few chapters of this book. For some, this may be enough for them to understand, while others may need to hear more about your personal experiences. If and when you feel comfortable, tell them your story. Ask them to listen to you without reacting or giving reassurance about how you look; ask that they just listen. If they're on board, perhaps they can help you with some of your exposures, just be a shoulder to cry on, or be a cheerleader for you. And if they're uncertain how to help, they can also seek out a therapist to help them help you.

We know it's difficult to be patient until your family understands BDD and learns the best way to support you in your recovery. In fact, we encourage you to pass this book on to them once you've finished reading it. Doing so will help them understand you and BDD better.

Overcoming BDD: The Next Steps in Your Journey

Throughout this book, we've congratulated you on your progress, because each step brings you closer and closer to that ultimate goal: overcoming BDD. At the beginning of your cognitive behavioral work, you probably felt that your BDD was in the driver's seat, cruelly laughing at you as you tried to take the wheel. With dedication to the cognitive and behavioral skills that we've offered in this book, you can push your BDD to the backseat, where it belongs. Continue to work to maintain the goals that you've achieved and the skills you've mastered. We wish that we could erase the troubles that BDD has caused you, and we wish even more that we could promise that you won't have to face these troubles again. However, what we can say with hearty confidence is that the skills in this book have empowered you to face your fears and take back what is rightfully yours: your self-worth and your happiness. Keep up the excellent work, and never give up on your life again.

References

Artnz, A., and A. Weertman. 1999. "Treatment of Childhood Memories: Theory and Practice." *Behaviour Research and Therapy* 11: 629–28.

Bögels, S. M. 2006. "Task Concentration Training versus Applied Relaxation, in Combination with Cognitive Therapy, for Social Phobia Patients with Fear of Blushing, Trembling, and Sweating." *Behaviour Research and Therapy* 44: 1199–1210.

Buhlmann, U., L. M. Cook, J. M. Fama, and S. Wilhelm. 2007. "Perceived Teasing Experiences in Body Dysmorphic Disorder." *Body Image* 4: 381–85.

Buhlmann, U., R. J. McNally, N. L. Etcoff, B. Tuschen-Caffier, and S. Wilhelm. 2004. "Emotion Recognition Deficits in Body Dysmorphic Disorder." *Journal of Psychiatric Research* 38: 201–6.

Buhlmann, U., R. J. McNally, S. Wilhelm, and I. Florin. 2002. "Selective Processing of Emotional Information in Body Dysmorphic Disorder." *Journal of Anxiety Disorders* 16: 289–98.

Buhlmann, U., and S. Wilhelm. 2004. "Cognitive Factors in Body Dysmorphic Disorder." *Psychiatric Annals* 34: 922–26.

Butters, J. W., and T. F. Cash. 1987. "Cognitive-Behavioral Treatment of Women's Body-Image Dissatisfaction." *Journal of Consulting and Clinical Psychology* 55: 889–97.

Campisi, T. A. 1995. "Exposure and Response Prevention in the Treatment of Body Dysmorphic Disorder." PhD diss., Hofstra University (Hempstead, NY).

Cash, T. F., B. A. Winstead, and L. H. Janda. 1986. "The Great American Shape-Up: Body Image Survey Report." *Psychology Today*, April, 20–37.

Deckersbach, T., C. R. Savage, K. A. Phillips, S. Wilhelm, U. Buhlmann, S. L. Rauch, L. Baer, and M. A. Jenike. 2000. "Characteristics of Memory Dysfunction in Body Dysmorphic Disorder." *Journal of the International Neuropsychology Society* 6: 673–81.

Didie, E. R., C. C. Tortolani, C. G. Pope, W. Menard, C. Fay, and K. A. Phillips. 2006. "Childhood Abuse and Neglect in Body Dysmorphic Disorder." *Child Abuse and Neglect* 30: 1105–15.

Eifert, G. H., and J. P. Forsyth. 2005. *Acceptance and Commitment Therapy for Anxiety Disorders: A Practitioner's Guide to Using Mindfulness, Acceptance, and Values-Based Behavior Change Strategies.* Oakland, CA: New Harbinger Publications.

Feusner, J. D., J. Townsend, A. Bystriksky, and S. Bookheimer. 2007. "Visual Information Processing of Faces in Body Dysmorphic Disorder." *Archives of General Psychiatry* 64: 1417–25.

Feusner, J. D., J. Yaryura-Tobias, and S. Saxena. 2008. "The Pathophysiology of Body Dysmorphic Disorder." *Body Image* 5: 3–12.

Gabbay, V., M. A. O'Dowd, A. J. Weiss, and G. M. Asnis. 2003. "Body Dysmorphic Disorder Triggered by Medical Illness." *American Journal of Psychiatry* 159: 493.

Geremia, G. M., and F. A. Neziroglu. 2001. "Cognitive Therapy in the Treatment of Body Dysmorphic Disorder." *Journal of Clinical Psychology and Psychotherapy* 8: 243–51.

Gunstad, J. and K. A. Phillips. 2003. "Axis I comorbidity in body dysmorphic disorder." *Comprehensive Psychiatry* 44: 207–276.

Hanes, K. R. 1998. "Neuropsychological Performance in Body Dysmorphic Disorder." *Journal of the International Neuropsychological Society* 4: 167–71.

Hayes, S. C. 2004. "Acceptance and Commitment Therapy and the New Behavior Therapies: Mindfulness, Acceptance, and Relationship." In *Mindfulness and Acceptance: Expanding the Cognitive-Behavioral Tradition*, edited by S. C. Hayes, V. M. Follette, and M. M. Linehan, 1–29. New York: Guilford Press.

Hayes, S. C., A. Masuda, R. Bissett, J. Luoma, and L. F. Guerrero. 2004. "DBT, FAP, and ACT: How Empirically Oriented Are the New Behavior Therapy Technologies?" *Behavior Therapy* 35: 35–54.

Hayes, S. C., D. Barnes-Holmes, and B. Roche, eds. 2001. *Relational Frame Theory: A Post-Skinnerian Account of Human Language and Cognition*. New York: Springer.

Hayes, S. C., and S. Smith. 2005. *Get Out of Your Mind and into Your Life: The New Acceptance and Commitment Therapy*. Oakland, CA: New Harbinger Publications.

Hayes, S. C., K. D. Strosahl, and K. G. Wilson. 1999. *Acceptance and Commitment Therapy: An Experiential Approach to Behavior Change*. New York: Guilford Press.

Heffner, M., and G. H. Eifert. 2004. *The Anorexia Workbook: How to Accept Yourself, Heal Your Suffering, and Reclaim Your Life*. Oakland, CA: New Harbinger Publications.

Holmes, E. A., and A. Mathews. 2005. "Mental Imagery and Emotion: A Special Relationship." *Emotion* 5: 489–97.

Jacobs, B., H. van Praag, and F. H. Gage. 2000. "Adult Brain Neurogenesis and Psychiatry: A Novel Theory of Depression." *Molecular Psychiatry* 5: 262–69.

Jerome, L. 1992. "Body Dysmorphic Disorder: A Controlled Study of Clients Requesting Cosmetic Rhinoplasty." *American Journal of Psychiatry* 149: 577–78.

Kabat-Zinn, J. 1990. *Full Catastrophe Living: Using the Wisdom of Your Body and Mind to Face Stress, Pain, and Illness*. New York: Random House.

Khemlani-Patel, S., F. Neziroglu, and L. Mancusi. 2011. "Cognitive Behavioral Therapy for Body Dysmorphic Disorder: A Comparative Investigation." *International Journal of Cognitive Therapy* 4: 363–80.

Kosslyn, S. M., J. Brunn, K. R. Cave, and R. W. Wallach. 1985. "Individual Difference in Mental Imagery Ability: A Computational Analysis." *Cognition* 18: 195–243.

Lambrou, C. 2006. "Aesthetic Sensitivity in Body Dysmorphic Disorder." PhD diss., University of London (England).

Levine, M. P., and L. Smolak. 2002. "Body Image Development in Adolescence." In *Body Images: A Handbook of Theory, Research, and Clinical Practice*, edited by T. F. Cash and T. Pruzinsky, 74–82. New York: Guilford Press.

Linehan, M. M. 1994. "Acceptance and Change: The Central Dialectic in Psychotherapy." In *Acceptance and Change: Content and Context in Psychotherapy*, edited by S. C. Hayes, N. S. Jacobson, V. Follette, and M. J. Dougher, 73–86. Reno, NV: Context Press.

Masuda, A., S. C. Hayes, C. F. Sackett, and M. P. Twohig. 2004. "Cognitive Defusion and Self-Relevant Negative Thoughts: Examining the Impact of a Ninety-Year-Old Technique." *Behaviour Research and Therapy* 42: 477–85.

McKay, D. 1999. "Two year follow-up of behavioral treatment and maintenance for body dysmorphic disorder." *Behavior Modification* 23: 620–629.

McKay, D., J. Todaro, F. Neziroglu, T. Campisi, E.K. Moritz, and J. A. Yaryura-Tobias. 1997. "Body dysmorphic disorder: A preliminary evaluation of treatment and maintenance using exposure & relapse prevention." *Behavior Research and Therapy* 35: 67–70.

Mulkens, S. 2007 (July). "Task Concentration Training in Body Dysmorphic Disorder." Presentation at World Congress of Behavior and Cognitive Therapies, Barcelona, Spain.

Mulkens, S., S. M. Bögels, and P. J. de Jong. 1999. "Attentional Focus and Fear of Blushing: A Case Study." *Behavioral and Cognitive Psychotherapy* 27: 153–64.

Mulkens, S., S. M. Bögels, P. J. de Jong, and J. Louwers. 2001. "Fear of Blushing: Effects of Task Concentration Training versus Exposure in Vivo on Fear and Physiology." *Journal of Anxiety Disorders* 15: 413–32.

Neziroglu, F, M. Hickey, and D. McKay. 2010. "Psychophysiological and self-report components of disgust in body dysmorphic disorder: The effects of repeated exposure. *International Journal of Cognitive Therapy* 3: 40–51.

Neziroglu, F, S. Khemlani-Patel, and D. Veale. 2008. "Social Learning Theory and Cognitive Behavioral Models of Body Dysmorphic Disorder." *Body Image* 5: 28–38.

Neziroglu, F., S. Khemlani-Patel, and J. A. Yaryura-Tobias. 2006. "Rates of Abuse in Body Dysmorphic Disorder and Obsessive Compulsive Disorder." *Body Image* 3: 189–93.

Neziroglu, F., D. McKay, J. Todaro, and J. A. Yaryura-Tobias. 1996. "Effect of Cognitive Behavior Therapy on Persons with Body Dysmorphic Disorder and Comorbid Axis II Diagnoses." *Behavior Therapy* 27: 67–77.

Neziroglu, F., D. McKay, J. A. Yaryura-Tobias, K. Stevens, and J. Todaro. 1999. "The Overvalued Ideas Scale: Development, Reliability, and Validity in Obsessive Compulsive Disorder." *Behaviour Research and Therapy* 37: 881–902.

Neziroglu, F., M. Roberts, and J. A. Yaryura-Tobias. 2004. "A Behavioral Model for Body Dysmorphic Disorder." *Psychiatric Annals* 34: 915–20.

O'Grady, A. C. 2002. "A Single Subject Investigation of Behavioral and Cognitive Therapies for Body Dysmorphic Disorder." PhD diss., University of Maine. *Dissertation Abstracts International: Section B—The Sciences and Engineering* 63(6-B): 3019.

Osman, S., M. Cooper, A. Hackmann, and D. Veale. 2004. "Spontaneous Occurring Images and Early Memories in People with Body Dysmorphic disorder." *Memory* 12: 428–36.

Pearson, A. N., M. Heffner, and V. M. Follette. 2010. *Acceptance and Commitment Therapy for Body Image Dissatisfaction: A Practitioner's*

Guide to Using Mindfulness, Acceptance, and Values-Based Behavior Change Strategies. Oakland, CA: New Harbinger Publications.

Phillips, K. A., E. Hollander, S. A. Rasmussen, B. R. Aronowitz, C. DeCaria, and W. K. Goodman. 1997. "A Severity Rating Scale for Body Dysmorphic Disorder: Development, Reliability, and Validity of a Modified Version of the Yale-Brown Obsessive Compulsive Scale." *Psychopharmacology Bulletin* 33: 17–22.

Rabinowitz, D., F. Neziroglu, and M. Roberts. 2007. "Clinical Application of a Behavioral Model for the Treatment of Body Dysmorphic Disorder." *Cognitive and Behavioral Practice* 14: 231–37.

Richter, M. A., S. Tharamalingam, E. Burroughs, N. A. King, W. E. Menard, J. L. Kennedy, and K. A. Phillips. 2004. "A Preliminary Genetic Investigation of the Relationship between Body Dysmorphic Disorder and OCD." *Neuropsychopharmacology* 29: S200.

Rodin, J., L. Silberstein, and R. Striegel-Moore. 1984. "Women and Weight: A Normative Discontent." *Nebraska Symposium on Motivation* 32: 267–307.

Salib, E. A. 1988. "Subacute Sclerosing Panencephalitis (SSPE) Presenting at the Age of 21 as a Schizophrenia-like State with Bizarre Dysmorphophobic Features." *British Journal of Psychiatry* 152: 709–10.

Saxena, S., and J. D. Feusner. 2006. "Toward a Neurobiology of Body Dysmorphic Disorder. *Primary Psychiatry* 13: 41–48.

Smolak, L. 2002. "Body Image Development in Childhood." In *Body Images: A Handbook of Theory, Research, and Clinical Practice*, edited by T. F. Cash and T. Pruzinsky, 65–73. New York: Guilford Press.

Smucker, M. R., and C. V. Dancu. 1999. *Cognitive Behavioral Treatment for Adult Survivors of Childhood Trauma: Rescripting and Reprocessing.* Northvale, NJ: Jason Aronson.

Sverd, J., J. Kerbeshian, G. Montero, S. Ferrante, and M. Donner. 1997. "Co-occurrence of Body Dysmorphic Disorder and Tourette's Disorder." *Psychosomatics* 38: 578–81.

Thomas, C. S., and D. P. Goldberg. 1995. "Appearance, Body Image, and Distress in Facial Dysmorphophobia." *Acta Psychiatrica Scandinavica* 92: 231–36.

Veale, D., A. Boocock, K. Gournay, W. Dryden, F. Shah, R. Willson, and J. Walburn. 1996. "Body Dysmorphic Disorder: A Cognitive Behavioural Model and Pilot Randomised Controlled Trial." *Behaviour Research and Therapy* 34: 717–29.

Veale, D., and F. Neziroglu. 2010. *Body Dysmorphic Disorder: A Treatment Manual.* Chichester, UK: John Wiley & Sons.

Vrana, S. R., B. N. Cuthbert, and P. J. Lang. 1986. "Fear Imagery and Text Processing." *Psychophysiology* 23: 247–53.

Wells, A. 2005. "Detached Mindfulness in Cognitive Therapy: A Metacognitive Analysis and Ten Techniques." *Journal of Rational-Emotive and Cognitive-Behavior Therapy* 23: 337–55.

Wells, A. 2000. *Emotional Disorders and Metacognition: Innovative Cognitive Therapy.* Chichester, UK: John Wiley & Sons.

Wild, J., A. Hackmann, and D. M. Clark. 2008. "Rescripting Early Memories Linked to Negative Images in Social Phobia: A Pilot Study." *Behavior Therapy* 39: 47–56.

Williams, J., T. Hadjistavropoulos, and D. Sharpe. 2006. "A Meta-Analysis of Psychological and Pharmacological Treatments for Body Dysmorphic Disorder." *Behaviour Research and Therapy* 44: 99–111.

Wilson, G. T. 2004. "Acceptance and Change in the Treatment of Eating Disorders: The Evolution of Manual-Based Cognitive-Behavioral Therapy." In *Mindfulness and Acceptance: Expanding the Cognitive-Behavioral Tradition*, edited by S. C. Hayes, V. M. Follette, and M. M. Linehan, 243–60. New York: Guilford Press.

Fugen Neziroglu, PhD, ABPP, ABBP, is a board-certified cognitive and behavior psychologist and leading researcher in the treatment of anxiety disorders, obsessive-compulsive spectrum disorders, trichotillomania, hoarding, body dysmorphic disorder and hypochondriasis at the Bio Behavioral Institute in Great Neck, NY, where she serves as director. She is also the coauthor of *Overcoming Compulsive Hoarding*, as well as *When Your Child is Cutting*. Her books have been translated to various languages.

Sony Khemlani-Patel, PhD, is a licensed clinical psychologist at the Bio Behavioral Institute in Great Neck, NY, where she specializes in the treatment and research of self-injury and obsessive-compulsive spectrum, anxiety, and mood disorders. She received her doctorate from Hofstra University in Hempstead, NY, and she has been practicing for more than 15 years in the field.

Melanie T. Santos, PsyD, is a licensed clinical psychologist at the Bio Behavioral Institute in Great Neck, NY, where she treats body image disorders.

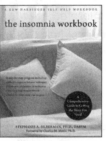
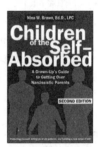